fore

CW00418783

I wrote this material when I w
if I'd ever have anything or an   ___ ___ _ _ _g
cared about. I don't want anyone to feel sorry for me or show
me anything that isn't by nature, "Nice." You're entitled to
your opinion, but I'll leave that with you. I've done my bit. I
am absolutely, irretrievably, undoubtedly, 100% honest in my
writing.

I've held back and I've been a liar for most of my life, but I
was really bad at it. I'm really tired of calling myself an
asshole knowing that I've either done nothing wrong or knowing
there is no way I could change, manipulate, or in any way make
myself look like a hero. What you are about to read is in many
ways my effort to show you how I think, what I think of myself,
what I've been told how others think of me and my perpetual
search for an understanding of myself and human nature.

This is me. This is who I am. Is there anybody out there?

—- *Joe Pollock*
August 30, 2020

If someone asked me why I wrote a book I would tell them: "I
don't write because I want to. I write because I have to. I
have no choice in the matter. I have to write just like I have
to eat, breath and sleep. I am a writer. Just like a fish has
to swim, a dog has to bark and a Chipotle has to give you food
poisoning, I'm a writer. It is my nature. I am an animal. A
creature. And that creature is a writer."

The work ethic is there. And most writers honestly don't even
have that. Most writers, like most artists in general, are
hoping that success will magically come to them. They hope that
someone will someday come knocking on their door in a nice
three piece Christian Dior with the Devil's contract in one
hand and a feathered quill in the other.

Hoping that for the measly price of a single soul, †
they can play the Hollywood Bowl, star in a Scorsese

Barnes & Nobles signing hardcovers as throngs of adoring fans file around the corner for their John Hancock.

They also have a definition of success that embodies something between George R. R. Martin, Stephen King, J.K. Rowling with all of the limelight, yet none of the workload. They see writing as a glorious endeavor, filled with red carpets. It is not. It's hard. It's not always fun. It sometimes feels like more editing than writing.

1 month to write the manuscript of the novel, 6 months to edit it. It's a tedious and monotonous process, to be honest. I'm not doing it to be the next E.L. James. I'm doing it because, as Karl Marx so elegantly stated, "A writer needs to eat to write, but a writer does not need to write to eat."

Writing is completely devoid of the success it may or may not carry. If that's why you write, then you're not a writer. You're a hungry journalist looking for a quick paycheck that you've convinced yourself is somehow easier than working a 9to5. It's not.

It may be less physically demanding than shelving boxes in an amazon warehouse but it is by no means devoid of monotony. Writing is laborious, and there are times when I truly hate it and wish that I could throw away the typewriter forever. It's a love-hate relationship that an artist has with his art.

Whether it be stand up comedy or dance; there are days where a dancer would love to throw away his dance shoes forever. There are days when a comic hates comedy so much that he could happily envision never stepping foot on a stage ever again. And that very thought fills his heart with glee.

Then there are other days where the comic thanks God that comedy exists, as the good lord has granted him an outlet, a therapeutic echo chamber in which he may pray away the sorrows and frustration amongst a house of his peers, it's like AA, only with more laughs, and a few more punchlines.

Writing can be fun and invigorating but it is by no means glorious. I don't even like writing most of the time. 2 and a 1/2 hours on 1 poem can be infuriating, especially when at the end of the 3rd hour, you're nowhere close to being done, and despite the fact that you keep reminding yourself that this poem will only fill 1 page, maybe a page and a half at best, you keep working on that same 1 poem because for 1 reason or another you're obsessed with the idea of perfection.

You won't be satisfied until all the words are in their proper places. It's like a jigsaw puzzle. You have the entire lexicon of human languages, and a plethora of slang and personal vernacular; and you have to organize, amongst billions of words, phrases, references, and metaphors; how it all fits together.

You beat yourself up because at some point you find yourself realizing that you don't know as many words as you thought you did. In fact, it seems as if all you know is 4 letter words and you wonder and start to worry if people will notice that you always use the same adjectives over and over and over again.

And so you get on thesaurus.com and you look through all the synonyms, hoping that the internet can help you not feel as dumb as you think you are. You think you're a fraud at times. you wonder, when you've gotten some minor or major praise or achieved some level of success, whether maybe you've pulled a magical trick.

Maybe you've pulled the wool over everyone's eyes and you're like The Wizard of Oz hiding behind a curtain, and someday soon Dorothy is going to expose you for being the fraud that you are. This is the mind of a writer. This is the mind of all artists.

And simultaneously while you're racking your brain, thinking you're terrible and a fraud, simultaneously you think you're the greatest thing since sliced bread, a truly impactful voice of a generation. You hate and love yourself simultaneously just like you love and hate your art simultaneously. You keep these 2 personalities inside you all the time. The egotist versus the nebbish questioner, an anxious nail biting, pessimist.

The writer can love his manuscript and hate it simultaneously. It's part of the reason why the writer needs others to read his writing, because between the egotist and the pessimist, he doesn't know how he feels about his own writing. 1 minute he could love his own draft, but he's never not but 1 negative comment or constructive criticism away from tossing it in the furnace and starting all over again.

—- *Robert Gold*
August 27, 2020

_____

_____

till death do us part

}

and in that hospital bed
you lay.

turning the sun,
the moon

and the stars
to gray.

in your life,
you mattered,

jess.
that glass ceiling,

you shattered it,
yes!

but now you sit here
a pool

of dark mattered
bliss.

in a comma'd rest.
soon your coffin

will be laid to rest.
gone from human stature,

fluttered off
into an empyrean portal.

shuffling off
this mortal coil.

off into heaven.
what happened to vegas,

and our 7 7 7 's.
we were so close

to retirement,
with pension checks

pilin[g].

my fuckin

sweet
sour

sorrowed
honey,

it's time to
exit stage right.

and i'll be absent my scene partner,
in the play that is life.

crying in our pimacott sheets,
wallowing in the night.

sighing over cotton seats,
swallowing the memory

of an undersmoked pipe.
remembering the legacy

of my favorite wife.
in my life i had four.

three of them were whores.
but you my baby,

you were more.
we had children,

we had four.
our life wasn't filled

with fighting
nor blood
nor gore.
we built a real estate empire,

yet started out poor.
you made a better man

out of me,
we complimented each other's

legacies.
building a team

that would make batman and robin jealous.
we were the best show on broadway,

better than sara bareilles.
baby,

sitting here with tubes
sticking out of you

left and right,
you still look

so fucking gorgeous.
but without you here,

i don't know what path
the future forges.

i hold your hand tight,
realizing that this is the very last bed

that i'll ever share with my wife.
future days

are going to be
far less sunny,

without my flour,
my apple,

my honey.
without you,

without my
partner-in-crime,

i don't know
if i'll be able to run

all these companies.
and spend all these hundies.

without you
it all just feels

like monopoly monies.
your life took on

such a pith.
now who will i have

to go on carnival cruises ships with?
but you lived a good life.

oh my sweet precious wife.
but with your consent.

i would stick
my stick.

in your mouth.
one last time.

_____
_____

die a hero or live long enough to see yourself become the
villain

_____
by robert gold
_____

when asked,
"when do lovers part,"
"when do armies retreat,"
 "when does the earth die,"
young men whisper never.
thinking that "they" will always be together.

in this manner young men are like kings, never realizing that
their empire is soon to cease to sing. and even when a council
of advisors advise the young men and kings, they laugh and
scoff and continue dawdling with their adolescent flings.

but neither realizes that just like how love turns to
heartbreak, times change, and empires fall. but nobody ever
plans accordingly for the final curtain call.

and not only do empires change, and not only does love change.
but individuals change. and ordinary men grow wicked, and wild,
and even strange. but nobody, especially not the kings or the
young men, take notice of this evolution of character that can
transpire in a given lifetime, and they don't realize that blue
can turn to red. and purple can turn to black, and love can
turn into a heart attack.

they don't think poets and priests can come from spoiled roots.
that hampton kin and beverly hills children can turn to boiled
brutes.

7

man's ability to change is part of the nature of our duality.
and it remains one of our fundamental principalities.

all things change, just as empires collapse.
and people fall away, out from our fingertips and grasp.
grapes turn to wrath, and mandela's turn a dark path.
mlk's turn away from a world of light and sunshine rays.
their hearts go gray, and they bleed on marble stones in the
ides of may.

fun dies, times churn like butter, generations begin as young
protesters against silly wars, and by their live's peroration;
they find themselves the elderly voters voting to send a new
generation of young protesters off to go fight more silly wars.

times change, like seasons. like clothes on a baby. the young
grow old
and become the very thing they laughed at and gave scold. we
become the very things we hate. old crotchety conservatives who
cease to have sex or masturbate.

young lovers never see past their own eyes. but that's only
because they're seeing the world through someone else's eyes.
they think the war on drugs is a big fat fuckin joke. but by
the time their elderly folk, they're voting for 20 year prison
sentences from marijuana, to meth, to coke.

they think patriotism is a thing their grandparents made up
during wwii and only applies when you're fighting nazis, when
you're fighting something that can be purely defined as pure
evil. but not every war is so black and white, not every enemy
looks dark against your light. not every moral principle can
hold a kite, to 50 years and marches, and progressive might.

relationships end. heartbreak descends. but in the moment when
everyone else around you is shouting, "get out! it's toxic.
it's no good, it's been bad from the very start." you just
laugh and turn to your lover, and show her the proof, "that the
world is trying to tear your love apart."

and so, like empires, funeral pyres, young lover's admirers,
kings, court jesters, and young protesters, you my dear reader
will whisper, "never."
even though nothing truly lasts forever.

and so when you ask an empire or a man at a funeral pyre, or a
young lover with a healthy admirer, or a king or a court
jester, or an old man or a young protester, "when do lovers

part, when do armies retreat, when does the earth die?" they
will whisper, "never." but you'll smile cause you know the
truth, that nothing truly lasts forever.

_____

_____

empire of the rising suns

_____

by robert gold

_____

the santa monica sand of summer's soothing grasp.
though as sunshine settles, the serenity shall not last.

the waves wash over my dampened toes.
but time will snatch this tempered abode.

the palm trees hummer with the hymns of sedation.
and the busy bees melody has found patience.

marble marshmallows, of the sapphire sky.
meeting the dark, and their empire dies.

tyrannical titans of the roman reach.
flags may flourish, from beach to beach.

but in the end.
all empires descend.
but we keep on loving,
again, and again and again.

_____

_____

~~legacy~~
aka
a semi autobiographical poem as told in words

_____

by robert gold

_____

the morale of this story
is that we suffer from mortal emotions.

and we can either accept it,
or be destroyed by it.

...emotions…

they can drive you
insane

like a stain
on the wooden floors

that you just can't rub out.
emotions,

they can rattle your brain
like a chain

on a prisoner
who might have been wrongly convicted.

emotions,
sometimes i ask myself

what do i gain
from this pain

inside my beating chest
that won't leave me alone.

and sometimes,
when i'm trying to sleep,

my dark thoughts
have dug too deep.

now they won't release me
from this prison

i call my cranium.
these steel walls of titanium.

it's all so shady.
and the road ahead is hazy.

it all seems like some
movie filled

drama nonsense.
humble experiences here

to protest.
life is hard,

never to know less.
i'm a saint,

i'm a sinner.
whatever picture

you wanna paint.
but anyway i figure

i can't anticipate
when hardships

gonna pull the trigger.
mine all started

when a girl decided to go.
and she's more amazing

than i'll ever know.
but these things called emotions

won't let the past fall
into the sands

of forgotten nightmares.
and this heart continuously tears.

we love to love.
it's an emotion like no other.

but sometimes
we forget

how much it costs.
it withers us away

in times of sorrow
and despair

in the wake
of a heart break,

so great.
the angels cried a tear for you.

but in times of luck and luxury
we can count on love.

it's forgiving and sweet.
unconditional

in arms of sweet embrace.

                    ...hate...

if we discuss love
then we must speak of hate.

the two are
inextricably tied

to one another.
and they can't

breathe
without each other.

in my hour of darkness.
she isn't standing

right beside me.
she's not speaking

words of wisdom
in my ear.

and she is absent
in the mirror.

and do you want to know why?
it's because she hates me.

she hates that i don't treat her like i used to.
she hates that i can't always give her 100% of my time.

she hates that i never say i love you anymore.
she hates that i don't try as hard to be romantic.

she hates
that we don't cuddle

in the cold night,
or any night,

for that matter.
so, i got lazy.

maybe it's cause we had a baby.
and though she'll always be my lady.

maybe.

i can't always be everything i was.

and it's not a simply just because.
i can't make your heart beat out of your chest for me.

but why can't you see?
that maybe.

i just wanted to grow old with you.
but hate got you too.

what kind of emotion got over you?
what kinda hate enveloped you?

and jealousy knows no other soul better than mine.
our attraction is so sublime.

i remember every time.
every action.

every motion.
every sense of pure devotion.

to:

                    ...jealousy...

i'm jealous.
i'm jealous of my brother.

who shares the blood of the father who raised us.
and i'm just some bastard that plagues us.

he's always been "the good son."
never given mom and dad

much grief.
it's my

honest belief.
and though i came out of some affair.

and for every reason i shouldn't care.
i wish these veins had your blood.

father that i know.
and not the father that didn't want me.

and not the father that never got to see.
what his mistake turned out to be.

because he wrote sonnets that made the angels cry.
and he wrote plays in the name of shakespeare.

and he wrote stories.
that rose to new modern glories.

because the millennials will shout my name.
because in this legacy i had my fame.

and all those who look down on me.
undoubtedly.

were around to see.
the audacity.

this bastard speaks.
reaching peaks.

higher than that vegas seven.
higher than heaven.

because this bastard boy was saved.
not by wealth or prominence.

but by love.

...Love...

earlier i said
we suffer from mortal emotions.

and sometimes
they create mistakes.

and sometimes
they bring new people into your life that brightens up the dark
road ahead.

my father did it for my mother.
and love would do it to any man.

and i've known hate.
and i've known jealousy.

but i still await the day when i'm going to love the way my
father has loved me.
a bastard who shares no relation.

and i know my father doesn't like it when i refer to myself
like that.
but sometimes when i look at how much better my brother is.

i feel like a bastard.
and i am jealous.

and i hold hate.
but in the end i love.

_____
_____
the greatest suicide story ever told
_____
by robert gold
_____

in her final letter,
she told me life would be better.

she wrote that i had nothing to offer.
oh how sweet, but a wonderful author.

fuck her. so i guess i meant nothing.
maybe the afterlife could offer that whore something.

she never even said a final goodbye.
well fuck her, i guess our love was a lie.

anyways. i danced with glee, what an utter illusion?
my family stared at me, in mesmerized confusion.

some friends tried to my console me, in my grief
and told me her depression was the true thief.

other friends told me i had a right to be angry at that cold
hard bitch.
i told them i bought her a life insurance policy, and now i'm
rich.

_____
_____
nathan bedford forrest
_____
by robert gold
_____

as southern culture crashes,
into dirt and dust.

a new soldier up arises,
believing he is just.

the phoenix dawns a hood
and a white cape with it too.

terrorizing jiggas,
and every single jew.

spawned out from the night.
lynching niggers & the kikes.

birthed out comes a fate.
black boys can't escape.

poplar trees bearing strange fruit.
there's blood on the leaves,
and blood on the root.

they string those black boys up,
the klu klux klan.

but white boy,
your heart of hate don't make you a man.

in the war of northern aggression,
i was a soldier and i marched with lee.
and i had control of the 7th cavalry.

but i don't take to terror so readily.
how will we rise, when we live on our knees?

maybe these preachers
have got a little point,
maybe it's peace
we oughtta anoint.

maybe this thing called bigotry
is a brain schism that we can lobotomize.

keep it buried deep and phosphorized.
in the earth and fossilized.

because i don't think it fits with me,
and i do not like it's synergy.

but i must be honest,

and tell the truth.

i'm as bad as custer
and as bad as booth.

i helped create this klan
before you that you see.

when i was young
and still naive,
i had a heart of hate in thee.

every day it stole from me,
a piece of soul, and salt.
and from the earth
i bore
a broken cult.

and from my mental womb
i bore a darkened heart.
and now i cry,
for the monster i created,
and the movement
i did start.

despite my turn from hate,
i cannot help but recognize,
the death that i create.

black boys hang
as their black bodies swing
in the southern breeze.
because of my misfortunes
and all of my misdeeds.

but maybe
there's hope for humanity.

if someone like thee,
can preach racial harmony,
and turn darkness to light,
and water from fire.
a former officer
of the confederate empire.

then maybe there's a maybe.
that this hate can be cured,
oh maybe there's a maybe.

that nothing is for sure.

and that all the men with faces,
are just paintings, nothing pure.

just look at this haggard beard.
i'm a picture perfect portrait
of man's ability to change.
and now all i need from you,
is for you to do the same.

_____
_____

zealot
_____
by robert gold
_____

i salute my poor dead brothers,
and my heart goes out to their southern gal mothers.

you know what…i should send home a letter.
to make my parents feel a little bit better.

dear mama,
it's april 18, 1865.
and i'm still alive.
sincerely,
nathan

ps: mama,
screw that
lincoln's emancipation proclamation
that he deems oh so right.
i heard a boy named booth
went ahead
and took his life.

now,
six months down the road.
i'm finally back home.

under occupation from yankee blues.
it's 6am, and we're out of food.

reconstruction amidst.
it's 6pm, we're out of shoes.

it's december now.
and we're freezin too.

but i reaffirm my solemn vow.
oh this land we will defend,
the south shall rise again.

_____

_____

the war in heaven

_____

by robert gold

_____

and then father cast you out,
like you were nothing.
but you could play the lyre, shape minds, change hearts,
you were something.

but you went against the word,
of the papa confessor.
thinking you could cast out,
your predecessor.

you foolish angel,
of bright allure,
you brought the answer,
but not the cure.

took up arms and wings,
and marched on heaven's gates.
now it's your little brother,
who sits-n-undulates.

at the right hand of heaven,
behind pearly gates.
holding the counterweights.
weighing the souls,
and eternal fates,
of these nail biting,
two legged primates.

these rejects of eden,
conniving and conceited.

rinsed and repeated.
drowned out, mistreated.
arc-less, they bleated.

and you,
thinking them your children too.
gave them promethean fire.
apples and education,
so that they may think higher.

you think,
you'd make to them
a better king,
a reign of peace
and parties,
and dance
and sing.

they'd be merry.
and cheery.
and no longer
face the wrath,
of father's fury.

and so,
you wait,
and plot,
and prance,
and plan.
smiling,
with malice,
as you furl your hands.

as you take his followers,
and they're conscious too.

whispering in papa's ear,
what will you do?
when there's no one left
to fight for you.

                   ————————————————
            ————————————————
      plagiarized from, i'm not racist by joyner lucas
                  ————————————————
                       by robert gold
                  ————————————————

character a:

the time period alludes to a poetic age in the lexicon of
americana.
before men sucked on each other's bananas.
in public view.

let's make america white again,
and forget all the gross indecent hedenstic trepidation's of
the kikes and the koons.
i'm not going to take cultural advice from a bunch of baboons.

i don't feel bad any time a nigger bites the bullet.
these cops ain't killers, they see the enemy and they pull it.

i'm not a feminazi,
i think you should feel shame for your body.

if you march onto thee, i'll tear you apart.
fuck your political correctness and your snowflake heart.

i think migits are migits, and gooks are gooks.
you ain't gettin me to read none of your sjw boo-ks.

i don't like no aliens landing their taco saucers and ufos on
my lone star.
you've swam far,

little jose,
but it's time to turn back the other way.

i hate hate, i really do,
i just think colors should not mix and mew.

character b:

why can't you open up your heart
to people who do not look like you?
why are you so close minded
and selfish too?

why is the idea of women having jobs
and self providing
and self describing
a pain on you?
and why does harvey milk
and lgbtq,
offend you?

nobody is asking you
to suck a dick.
there just asking you
to be slightly less of a prick.

queer love,
black love,
trans love,
interfaith love,
love is love.

and the
downtrodden,
beaten,
broken,
bones,
of the silent minority
have had enough.

because that
silent minority,
an intersectional
american sorority,
are quickly becoming
the loudest majority.

their political stance,
won't shy away from people like you.
we beat the nazis once,
and we'll do it for you.
we beat the fascists once,
now it's time for round two.

---

first they came

by robert gold

---

first they came for the natives and you didn't speak out.
because you weren't a native.

then they came for the africans, and you did not speak out,
because you weren't an african.

then they came for the mexicans, and you didn't speak up, you
weren't mexican.

but then they came for you, and there was no left to fight for
you.

---

the blossom beats for no unborn

by robert gold

---

every song on the radio is about us.
every cloud in the sky is a god given portrait of us.

every movie is about us.
every poem is about us.

every play is about us.
the faces of our friends.

they're all fun, and we share them.
they are like children, in an untitled wedding vow.

but the blossom beats for no unborn.
the rhythms of the rain, like teardrops from the heavens.

fall like fire upon a sieging castle.
hailstones upon harmony.

what orchestra used to play.
now the conductor is dead.

the trains were stopped on its tracks.
and you just keep telling me to relax.

_____
_____

dear andrew

_____

by robert gold

_____

dear andrew,

blood of my blood.
through dirt and shit and mud.

even when i leave you with a bittersweet taste.
you embrace.

i've abused you.
used you.
and i feared that i'd lose you.
but your unconditional adulation.
filled with patience.

is more than i have ever given you.
oftentimes my love has been aloof.

born of the same mother.
i am proud to call my brother.

sincerely,
your older brother
robert

_____
_____

blue gum blood

by robert gold

i left my home and friends to battle with the foe.
to save the southern land from misery and woe.

braved the potomac and appomatox with robert e. lee.
hoping war would make something of a man out of me.

i rode with the northern virginia with my springfield in my
hand. and for the southern land, i spilled yankee and blue gum
blood, on pennsylvania sand.

death became me as i rode my horse upon thee.
in the last battle of the war, my belly was torn.

and as 300,000 blues came marching to the appomattox court
house under general grant. a cobalt 45 pierced my belly fat.

i looked up and saw the angels crying. i asked why, and they
said, they were weary, to the sight of fratricide.

philosophers of prosperity

by robert gold

hateful voices cloud my vision and my heart boils as my ears
are pierced with the clatter of kike. old remnants of the third
reich.

though i was under the impression that these serpents of
ceremonial slaughter lost their place in the world a good
seventy years ago.
but some still walk that road.

and remain in their volatile mode.
a dead era's episode.

and yet the darkness follows me and all the rest like a
vulture.
and we can't seem to love one another's culture.

truthfully, i probably sound like some hippy.
trying to relive 1960.

can i bestow on you a flower upon your gun?
a perfect pacifistic empire of the sun.

and now i'm lost in the disillusion that there may truly be no
hope.
when all i'm lookin at is three little black boys at the end of
their rope.

i'm disgusted by what i see.
what hate prospered in the 20th century.

in a world of frauds and fakes.
were prone to so many god awful mistakes.

and i know i can't be the only soul that shakes.
witnessing the red rivers humanity makes.

just look back once upon a time.
before the raps, the riddles and the rhyme.

when our dear earth was pure.
and we didn't need some clean energy cure.
i'm sincerely unsure.

if its creationism.
or just sensationalism.

and god damn it why don't i have
all the prescriptions to my problems.

you answer me that oh dear holy father?
no you're not even listening, you won't even bother.

i'm just trying to get back to the days of cane and abel.
before europe went unstable.

when we had purity.
and some sense of security.

when the garden of eden nourished adam and eve.
before the satanic serpent showed his sinful sleeve.

before napoleon rose to power.
and burnt down king louie's tower.

before the movie pictures, the poetry and the plays.
before woodstock rolled their blunts to blaze.

before david played the harp, in the name of the lord.
before achilles stayed in troy, and claimed fame with a sword.

once upon a day.
 before industrialization transformed the world to gray.

it is the legacy we chose to sow.
before ivory became ebony's foe.
a long long time ago.

before spartacus changed the game.
and claimed rome's fame.

it was inked into permanence with the theological biblical
text.
that put popes to rest, and made sinners confess.

now tmz tells us when the sun will set.
and cnn will tell us when charlie sheen's upset.
in the age of the internet.

now the 21st century shines a new light.
as humanity struggles to find what's right.

and i look around me and all i see is a rumbled america in a
new age new era. blood stained stripes in the mirror.

my feet are planted in the solemn steps of my red white and
blue.
in the star spangled banner that i once knew.

wealth's to the wastelands of the third world war.
black golds is what we decided to die for.

and as i stand here.
shedding my patriotic tears.

in the irony of the truth that we are not slaughterers.
and it's not the legacy of our founding fathers.

to live in this burned out body of battered earth.
of where i share my birth.

because now only death and destruction rule the day.
so why do i stay?

as the ramparts were so gallantly streaming.
saying their last goodbye to the twilight's last gleaming.

as i behold the silver star crafts leaving.

colonization opportunities beaming.

as they sail on their voyage.
i'll stay here.

in the only world i've ever known.
while others fly away across the cosmos.
where nobody knows those.

who sang the harlem blues.
and liberated the jews.

america the beautiful with your gracious skies.
and your amber eyes.

in the land of the brave.
where that star spangled banner may yet still wave.

this soil is all of me.
my whole hearted history.

marauders and mystery.
in this life i was jolly.
but here i stand melancholy.

america, my darling, you're the only home i ever knew.
and the truth is, i don't know what to do.

so this is the story of human creation.
in the dawn of the american nation.

malcolm x once said that we must always live separately.
because we will never live equal.

because in a world of distrust.
the white man will never be just.

and every word that he spews from his serpentine lips, is a
word he lied to us. and ever absurdly, takes us further from
the truth, is another right he denied to us.

we can never live side by side.
as brothers and sisters.

so now i ask you this question.
do you believe his philosophies, true?

have the decades since proved him wrong?

is the 21st century singing a new song?

can mortal men change their chord?
because my feet can't carry me far enough lord.

and this soul can't stay bound to this mortal world lord.
and the cold unforgiving hatred in this world is all i've ever
known.
constantly living with sins we can never atone.

and the people of this mortal coil have called me a mick, lord.
and they've called me a spic, lord.

but what they don't know is that the blood that runs in these
veins is so much more than just black or white.
it's red, white and blue.
it's as green as the prairies and pastures made out of you.

though some with not as much faith in your creations.
would have us believe.

that humanity.
it's made out of insanity.
that comes out of genocidal vanity.

and i remember the great memphis pastor.
and his great words of wisdom.

as he preached about the freedom that would rain from the hill
tops of georgia. washing away the injustice the world bore yah.

i listened to his speech.
 and the future he sought to reach.

i see it in this world today.
and maybe were not so utterly gray.

and i was thinking about it.
how he was quoting lincoln no doubt.

as he spoke of the fourscore
and seven years ago.

singing sweet land of liberty.
america, tis of thee.

because no matter what lies remain in society.
man comes in a thousand shapes and varieties.

you can say it's the texture that lays upon our skin.
but it's not the culprit of our sin.

you can say it a thousand times.
but it's not the colors that commit the crimes.

the pastor talked about a great american.
who simply tried to act a good samaritan.

signing the emancipation proclamation.
and without hesitation.

the world put two bullets in their heads.
and they were laid down to rest in their coffin beds.

just like mahatma gandhi, malcolm x and two of the kennedy's.
the world paid them back for their peaceful obscenities.
setting flames to their ideological serenity.

so let me ask you now, lord.

is my soul sinful and sorrowful and bound for hell?
because sometimes i feel like you and i are just strangers who
just happen to know each other very well.

is this my fateful destiny that is to be unfurled?
the deepest darkest depths of your dark angel's underworld.

but lord i hope that even in the flaws of humanity.
you look past our vanity.
and our constant insanity.

past the blood stain of russian marxism.
past our racism.
and the corrupt system.

past our war.
and the vietnam boys we sent off to do lbj's tour.

please forgive our politically incorrect politicians.
and even our desert storm missions.

because i don't know if we'll ever stop sinning?
and realize that war isn't winning.

because what we currently consider to be victory.
it's truly sick to me.

it's time to find our unity.
i have a rhyme in mind for impunity.
to give our sinners their immunity.

do the heavens cry crocodile tears to appear right?
or do they truly want us to unite?

did you make us like this on purpose, lord?

flawed and inflamed.
the pacifists waiting off to the side, ashamed.

there are so many roads of possibility yet explored.
cause i see a day when we can be better, lord.

the centuries are changing us.
remedies for the hatred and disgust.
turning old conflicts to dust.

as bombs burst, turning the world to vapor.
this pen will forever fix words to paper.

cause i'm spreading the gospel of peace, sire.
heading towards the race war's ceasefire.

because one day we may finally see.
the end to this infinite fallacy.

the long awaited day when the bullets are a relic.
do the war torn not cry for a day so angelic?

a day when we can speak of great history.
and look back on our glorious legacy.

and with honest sincerity.
i title this poem, philosophers of prosperity.

because the generations remember the names
lincoln and they remember doctor king.

for as history has shone.
their names are carved in stone.

even after they've turned from ash and bone.
their legacy will forever sit upon it's holy throne.

and though the assassin's bullet stole these philosophers from
us while their song was young. their legacy will forever remain
an empire of the sun.

and just like us, the children of our children will sing your
songs too.
and forever they'll remember you.

and as long as there are teachers to teach.
and preachers to preach.

poets to poeticize.
and romantics to romanticize.

the words of great individuals will never go unheard.
and their message will never die.

because as history would have it their legacy was meant to
last.
and nobody will forget the philosophers of the past.

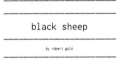

black sheep

by robert gold

i live in south central,
the gangster's metropolis.
it's a poet's apocalypse.

just a sixteen year old boy,
with a glock in my sock.

but i'm not one for capone,
i be chillin with whitman.

more kindred to the words of buddha.
cuz when i look in the mirror all i see is neruda.

while the rest of the homies,
roll up blunts to blaze.

i be watchin the tonys,
cuz i want to write plays.

me and my homies,
we slingin coke,
that's no joke.

i just do what i do,
cuz you survive with a crew.

i'm not hard thru and thru,
but i keep a gun in my shoe.

don't think me gestapo,
i'm one for picasso.

langston hughes,
is my muse.

it's plato, i'll choose.
though i'll go for some homer,
and soft rock blues.

i think rob frost is a boss,
in poe i get lost.

when you lower the curtain,
the page is my purpose.

and i'll keep rapping and rhyming,
again and again.

to shove off the pain,
and break from these chains!

_____

_____

her breasts
_____

by robert gold
_____

her lipstick, her glass.
her chest, her ass.

her lips are fine wine, and her kisses are like silk.
with eyes like sapphires and skin like diamonds.

her beauty is all mine.

i admire the freckles spread like parchment across the
conclemation of her face.
and when her head rests upon my chest, i can hear my heart
beating at 90 miles per hour.

the feel of her breasts,
cupped in my hands.

the way her lipstick kisses her glass,
every time she takes a sip.

the way her skirt brushes against her thighs.

her tongue,
dancing like fire,
as it moves.

her fingertips,
prickling across my chest,

as she graces me with the serenity of her touch.

the sexiness of her step.
the way her hips hug her jeans.

if i denied her beauty,
it would be all but lies.

_____
_____

atheist poetry so that darwin's ghost
has something to rub it out too

_____
by robert gold
_____

when the universe was yet an unborn child.
standing in the darkness of her mother's womb.
before light came upon the utter nothingness.
when the spark of humanity was still eons away.

the rock and the rubble beneath our feet.
beauty procured after only 13 billion years of ticking clocks.
now the rain falls from the clouds.
and the wind whistles from the clouds.

imagine a sky with no stars.
think of an ocean with no drop of water.
not even a fish in the sea.
no evolutionary trace of you or me.

soon, what we know as truth today.
in the realms of modern science.
would form in mother earth's fingertips.
as the puzzle pieces began to take their shape.

the energy that surrounds our eyes.
the first energy to know the universe.
this energy breathed life into the subatomic particles.

and these particles became protons and neutrons and electrons.

bringing us one step closer to the world we know today.
planets took shape as matter condensed.
clusters of stars shifted.
and gas giants screamed thunderous roars.

like a fresh painter.
 onto a white canvass.
the big bang colored the galaxy with colored
fireworks across the skies of cold space.

the atoms found their way into the surface.
wearing the masks made of hydrogen.
and suits with helium bow ties.
and lithium button-ups.

the elements that once knew no name.
began to synthesize within the supernova.
and the giant clouds formed stars.
the ones we know in the telescope today.

the incarnation of how it all
came to pass is still a vast mystery.
but it's believed that as matter condensed.
it caused a great expansion.
and that is how it came to pass.

_____
_____

dead poet's society

_____
by robert gold
_____

all i do all day is throw raps and rhymes together.
my worries are weightless, and light as a feather.
so i spent the hours of my hourglass tryna be better.

when i had a bad day.
this is what i say.

grab your palms, have a moment of zen.
now you're calm, so you pick up the pen.

write a tune.
real soon.
about a balloon, goon, rune or the moon.

systematically it's a simplification.
an aristocratically overstepped generalization.

34

but democratically we've found your patience.

started low.
now there you go!

what masterpiece comes next...?
i want to see the rest!

every artist!
works their hardest!

to see themselves known!
to see their art shown!

oh my advice may make you groan, and moan and moan.
but when you're famous, you'll ring me on the telephone!

and your apologies may well atone.
for the success that i have sown!

it isn't right! it isn't right! dreadfully long days drag to
the night!
oh no! you're almost out of fight!

you've lost your bark, and you've lost your bite!
and your spark! it's almost out of light.

but a writer will write...and write...and write and go and go
and go.
that's the only truth the poets know.
(*mic drop)

---

in the sun that meets the moon

---

by robert gold

---

in the heart of every poet.
in the heart of every artist.
there's a story to be told.
and there's a tune to be played.

in the mind of every man.
in the practice of every preacher.
there's a legacy to be written.
and there's a sermon to be spoken.

in the heart of every lover.
in the heart of every crush.

there's lust to languish in,
and there's daydreams to be dreamed.

in the philosophies of every prophet.
in the teachings of every teacher.
there's followers to be had.
and there's points to be punctuated.

in the might of every god.
in the campaign of every conqueror.
there's a power to be stirred.
and there's a boy to be embattled.

in the light of every shadow.
in the sun that meets the moon.
there's a deep that meets the shallow.
and there's a hope in all the darkness.

———————————————
———————————————

kira

———————————————

by robert gold

———————————————

`you stack more cups, then a boob job surgeon.
you feel so tight, must be a virgin.

spend more time in the sheets than the klu klux klan.
we fuck all night, make me feel like a man.

you reject more advances than a stalingrad frontline.
get more calls then a hot bling hotline.

you've had more bitches than michael vick.
you've taken more licks then a lollipop stick.

you're a kobe bryant slam-dunk.
and you got more funk
then 90s punk.

and now it's time to say goodbye.
i guess that means this is my very last rhyme.

———————————————
———————————————

a muse, to the artists
&
the best groupie god ever gave
birth to

———————————————

by robert gold & joe pollock

———————————

you're my muse.
and beauty knows no other soul,

better than you.
because you're the best thing,

that i ever knew.
your my mocha chocolate,

my nappy-headed queen,
my phat ass princess,

and my personal dose of lean.
you're the heart throb.

you could stop traffic, and inspire elvis presley not to die on
the toilet,

 like a pussy.
and all the while make him go crazy
with that nubian tushy.

and you make my heart stop.
you're the blind watchmaker.

a goddess in human skin,
come down to earth to give me a job on the rim.

you're a catch. with a nice sweet pineapple tasting snatch.
i think it's because you eat so much pineapple.

which, apparently, is supposed to make your vagina taste good.
what a team player, to give me a fruity tasting snatch, my
sweet little sour patch.

you're a purple quartz gem.
and you're different from all of them.

and when i say them, i mean other bitches.

you're the correct selection.
you're my ball of perfection.

you're my boo bear, and my blue butterfly.
you make all the other poets cry.

every single fucking one of them.

and when i say other poets,
i mean other guys you fucked.

because you're an inspiration.
to the artists of the nation.

you could turn harvey milk not gay.
you could get anthony bourdain not to kill himself.

you could make the dali lama give up veganism,
and make hitler not racist.

you could make andrew dice clay funny.
actually, scratch that, you're not a miracle worker.

you could inspire napoleon to win waterloo.
lee at gettysburg. you're the muse that puts men on the moon.

and the drug that weans heroin addicts off of the brink.
you're like gandhi, if gandhi was cool.

they are not worthy of your advice.
but thank god they have it anyway
.

even though most of them are not worthy of your presence or
your words or your grace.

you could get shakespeare to write a romeo and juliet sequel,
with your pussy, just one taste.

———————————————
———————————————

a song of fire and ice
———————————————
by robert gold
———————————————

the moon, the sun and the stars fell out of the sky when i met
you.
we were so young, and naive, and for years i've loved you from
a

distance. i've watched you bring home guy after guy after guy,
every single night. and still i think thoughts of love about
you,

never telling you what i feel or how i want you, i think these
thoughts but i keep them to myself. admiring your edges, your

hedges, your ridges. your curves, your spine, like a hardcover
book upon a shelf. oh your back, your hips, your thighs, oh how
i'd

love to make you mine. love and me were but simply
acquaintances before you breathed meaning into my life.

like a kid's kite, or an opium flight, i need you now, i need
you tonight. swoop into my life, it hurts too much, i need you
right now.

i know how it sounds, but everyday i imagine you in a wedding
gown. i can't stop. i can't help myself. i can't control the
mr. hyde,

inside, forever. i've been dr. jekyll, controlling my peckle.
but any longer, and the love inside of me is going to explode
like

an atomic bomb on hiroshima. or the acting career of john cena.
building up like a volcanic eruption, i need to be able to
squirt,

like a brazzers porn star, i need to burst. i must steal you
now! now! like a viking. kidnap you and ravish you like bill
cosby.

i want to have you and hold you all through the night. with
spanish fly, i'll warm your body on a cold night. as long as
you keep that

pussy tight. you & i will be alright. i love you with hot
passionate fire. fire that burns hotter than a thousand suns. i
love you more

then rednecks love jeff foxworthy and ar-15 guns. i love you
like a thot for hire, like sourdough buns. i think it would be
fun. if i just

bent you over the pulpit and took you like a catholic nun. i
love you so much i don't even care that you slept with every
member

of our high school varsity water polo team. and put it up
online as xxx d.p. if that's what you want. to have men inside
your ears,

your nose and your cont. who am i to judge, i'm no saint.

i'm not the perfect picture you'd want to paint. not a chapel

boy, not a 10 out of 10 on the morality scale. i'm no slut shamer,
or lion tamer. you be you, and i be me. because your sex love

positivity, is absolutely fine with me. you can suck off
homeless guys in the home depot parking lot, for all i care,
fuck gigolos and

nightclub bouncers and football jocks, at the end of the day it
doesn't matter how many men enter your maiden head. we'll still

have our bed. i know at night, i'll be the only walrus
ravishing you at midnight. what i never knew before i met you,
is that we don't

choose love. it takes every man by storm. what i have felt. is
not something all are privy to. although my romantic
attractions for

you have been afar, and i've watched you suck off a walmart
employee in your car. you have given me the only thing worth

living for. even the promise of a possible future together
someday fills my belly, my stomach, and my heart with
adulation, glee and

puts a skip in my step. and gives me a reason to get out of bed
in the morning. you are my life, my soul, my everything. i just
wish

that we could be together. too bad you're my sister.

_____
_____

the graduate
_____
by robert gold
_____

my $250 an hour therapist lied.
the legacy of love never dies.

the heartbreak i feel,
feels like it'll never end.

nearly 3 or 4 years ago,
on my knees i prayed for cupid.
and for a while he bestowed upon me bliss.

but post-relationship.
but post-break up.
post-love.
post-romance.
post-happiness.

i look in the mirror and my eyes bleed.
a pool of tears and my heart seethes.

love is unforgiving, absent the subtle touch of desire.
and the beat of my heart is set to fire.

yet every time i try to live in infatuation's perpetuated
perfection.
never does happiness become the humble word of mention.

so i end up melancholy's recurring patient.
the strings of my soul, handcuffed to the hazards of damnation.

an eternity intertwined,
tethered romance.

a fate of simple presentation that emerges itself
as if to be a silent orchestra.

on a road unfound.
drumming forever on it's bittersweet sound.

reminding me of what used to be.
and i can't seem to find the one that replaces your memory.

what is lost to the broken of a once great empire,
lays a ruined mass of a truthful liar.

feeding my soul the secrets of your past.
now stands an ancient hourglass.
bringing us closer, was i foolish to think that love could ever
last?

the thought of never seeing you again makes my heart weak, my
thighs numb, my stomach sick, and my eyes cry.
just because i fucked your mom, doesn't mean we have to say
goodbye.

_____
_____

prop 8

_____
by robert gold
_____

victor.
oh god, that sex crazed victor.

a hot young latin.
with the body of an assassin.

because if looks could kill.
victor would be a serial killer.

he's just that sexy.
my olive little mexi.

but unfortunately.
the straight folk wanna give us marriage.

how god damn inconsiderate of them?
because although victor may be a hottie.

i can't marry victor.
he ain't marriage material.

we probably have a couple good months left at best.
so calm on carpet munchers, give it a fuckin rest.

i mean, don't get me wrong.
victor and i have sung a good song.

he's a suckable friend.
and a fuckable one, amen.

and did i mention?
his 12 inch cock is perfect.

but if this prop 8 bullshit passes.
victor's going to want to get married.

i thought this day would never come.
i was completely satisfied just drinking his cum.

i couldn't stand a lifetime in his presence.
oh my god, as a husband he'd be a menace.

i'd rather have a wife.
then have another year of victor in my life.

so if gay marriage becomes legit.
everyday with victor is going to be shit.

———————————————————

jekyll

———————————————————

by robert gold

———————————————————

and even though you don't like any of the other fish in the
sea.
you've taught me how to love & hate something simultaneously.

you killed me and crucified me,
you stilled me and deified me,

you yin me then you yang me.
and sometimes you sang to me.

but you're the devil on the fourth horse.
or maybe you're an angel straying me on the right course.

i don't know if your darkness, or light.
sometimes you're a bullet, and sometimes you're a kite.
but you force me to sleep with one eye open, every single
night.

your jekyll, your hyde, your malevolence cannot be denied.
but neither can your kindness. your highness.

you're my queen, you're my tyrant.
like black lives matter, you make me go silent.

you make me scream and shout,
you make me quieter than a mouse.

you're joker, your batman.
you're skinny, you're the fat man.

your duality is complex to me. you have good and evil
tendencies.
you're god and your lucifer simultaneously.

you're bonnie and clyde,
but you're also the law man.

you're a bank robber,
and a fbi officer.

you wake up angry,
throwing plates across the room.
you wake up happy,
laying breakfast plates on my morning lap.

you wake me with kisses,
you wake me up with crucifixes.

you're a bitch,
you're my best friend.

you're a cunt,
you're a messiah.

you're a fucking genius,
you're the dumbest person i've ever met.

you're black, you're white.
your hitler, your gandhi.
you're dixie chicks,
but you're also gwen stefani.

oh my sweet jess.
you're no different from all the rest.

you're unlike any relationship i've ever been in, you're a
bipolar mess.
like i'm dealing with a social worker who doubles as a pillow
princess.

you're a jew,
you're a nazi.

you're baseball,
you're yahtzee.

you're a catholic.
you're a satanist.

you're the high school rapist,
you're the nurse,

the counselor,
the principal,
and the high school's founder.

you're a philanthropist,
and a serial killer.

you're an earthquake.
and the building's pillars.

you're a vampire stake.
and the vampire's killers.

your dracula.
your frankenstein.

you're the town slut,
and you're all mine.

your the mascot,
and the emo cutter.

your l.b.j.
and the school bully.

your mlk.
and george lincoln rockwell.

your lorraine bobbit.
and johnny sins.

you're a fourth wave feminist.
your milo yiannopolous.

you kiss me,
then punch me.

you kick me,
then love me.

you break up with me,
and then call me crying.

you tell me you never wanna see me again,
you tell me you wanna get back together again.

you tell me you're getting back with your ex.
then you tell me you wanna have my babies.

you're volatile,
you're irresistible.

you're marriage material.
you taste like copper cereal.

you're prometheus.
you're the flood.

you're water.
you're mud.

you're a couch potato.
and a mover.

your al capone.
your j. edgar hoover.

you're e.l. james.
you're the poetic edda.

you're garbage.
and you taste like feta.

you're stephanie meyers.
you're robert louis stevenson.

you're fires.
you're oxygen.

you're natural beauty.
you're collagen.

7 years down the road.
we've tied the knot, and share an abode.

now that we're married.
we have 4 children together.

but you're still a cinder block.
and you're still a feather.

i love you,
i hate you.

you make me wish i was gay.
every single fucking day.

_____
_____

the devil's diary
_____
by robert gold
_____

be the god of your own life. give out love like the precious
currency that it is. destroy your insecurities. destroy your
low self esteem. destroy the image of all the haters who said
you weren't

worth it. because you are so fucking worth it. you must
surround yourself only with those who love you as much as you
love them! don't let your heart be a whore to resistant hearts.
your heart is a

flower and it deserves to be watered! destroy those in your
path that take glee in your troubles.
ignorant people and moronic heathens of the earth aren't worth
a penny. and you must not lift a

finger to lift them off the ground from which they belong!
vanquish the false gods of abraham and all their preaching
pretenders! peddling salvation and a book of lies meant to
chain you up and rid

you of all that makes you beautiful, artistic, sexual and
sensual. you're a fuckin god in human flesh and deserve to be
autonomous! autonomous from the rules of yesterday, set forth
by long dead goat

herders! manipulate yourself to believe in yourself. fake it
until you make it. if you're not a confident conquering badass
bitch, play the part and eventually the shoes will fit! the
world is a god damn

stage and your a fucking actor! you're the shakespeare of this
kingdom and it's time to own the role.
you're not a scared little duckling, your a fucking goddess!
you're lilith! you're lucifer! you're eve

in the garden, telling god to go fuck himself because you're
gunna eat that fucking apple and taste what it means to be
human for the first time in your fucking life. because your not
gunna let some

patriarch in the sky tell you who to fuck, and who to marry and
who to love. you're the master of the garden, and you're naked
… but for the first time in your life … you're not afraid of
the world that lies

… outside the garden.
_____
_____

to the tune of, i feel like i'm fixin to die a rag
_____
by robert gold
_____

and it's a one two, can't you see all these mothers are oh so
blue?

47

and it's a one two, but all we got was closed eyed boys for
you.

welcome to your four year tour.
what are we fighting for?

commies just can't be ignored.
and it's a three four, tell me why are we in this war?

and it's a three four, love died with the napom of 64.
and now i just don't give a damn.

registering with uncle sam.
now i'm off to viet-nam.

and it's a five six, pickin up those ammo sticks.
and it's a five six, nothin a lil ak can't fix.

give that cut a few quick licks.
here for those top chief pricks.
did the charlie babies take some good hard kicks?

and it's a seven eight, and so how many more at this rate?
and it's a seven eight, bringing boys to fight from every
state.

dying next to your good old fashion mates.
golden crowns and pearly gates.
shedding blood for coffin fates.

and it's a nine ten, and now soon it'll be war time again.
and it's a nine ten, surrounded by all these lying old men.

melancholy with my paper and pens.
because coming home, i don't know when's.
well lbj, it just depends.

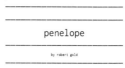

penelope

by robert gold

now it's me and penelope. we're gonna cruise with the millions.
love is ours to conquer. we are on top of the world.

and nobody can knock us down. every moment is a moment to
remember.
when it's the cold of december. she makes it feel like a summer
in july.

48

without her i would die. with her i will prosper. and if i ever
lost her. it would be my descension. tell me, did i mention?
it's me and penelope forever.

i'll barely cheat on you at all. and i promise,
i won't even make you raise the kid completely by yourself.

i won't even hit them, or spank them, or lay hands on them.
because i know, you're a kinky bitch, and you'd get jealous.

spanking and slapping and ropes and leather and biting and
choking would be our language of love. so much so, that if i
spanked our daughter, you'd consider it cheating.

for an eternity our passionate bdsm love will last. we'll be
fucking and fucking until the day we die. in truth, i hope that
if you marry me someday, that we will die fucking.

i love you so much i want the last thing i ever do, is to cum
up, inside of you. or perish in the attempt. because what
better way to leave this earth. then the way that i did on the
day of my birth.

i entered this world through a vagina, actually … no … well …
kinda-uh. i have a big head, so it was actually a c-section.
sorry … i… uh … forgot to mention.

sadness never envelopes the soul when you are near. you
brighten the darkest depths of the ocean. you illuminate the
dark cave that is my desperation. and from your booty, i feel
in thee, i feel the constapation.

———————————————————
———————————————————

to the tune of, when johnny goes marching home
———————————————————
by robert gold
———————————————————

why are these mothers all so blue
hurrah hurrah
we paid for your boys and caskets too
hurrah hurrah
we did it all for lbj
hoping those commies would go away
but there's 50 thousand dead at the end of the day
it took ten years to lose the war
hurrah hurrah
they drafted us
we did our tour

red, white and blue
it's always pure
hurrah hurrah
and the star spangled banner waves for-e-ver moooooooooooooore.

_____

_____

her body stood naked
_____

by robert gold
_____

the moon was horny that night.
as it peaked it's ugly eye upon my window sill.

i laid naked with olive tanned abdominals sweating.
my teeth biting at my pillow as i waited for her.

in my bed i waited in lustful anticipation.
holding my package in hand as it awaited delivery.

as the bathroom door opened, there stood her.
she was only gone for but a moment.

but in her return.
her body stood naked.

her thighs were wet with desire.
begging for my lushes thrusting stallion.

soon, oh so very soon.
my horny pony would ride to the promised land.

as the windows of my soul gazed upon her elegance.
i noticed the absence of a bushel.

she was but a shaven princess, with not a hair in sight.
oh what a relief, i awaited a hairless dinner tonight.

_____

_____

a science fiction poem better than douglas adams, orson scott
card & l ron hubbard combined
_____

by robert gold
_____

in this burned out body of battered earth.
of where i share my birth.

death and destruction rule the day.
so why do i stay?

starships gleaming.
opportunities beaming.

away across the cosmos.
where nobody knows those.

who sang the harlem blues.
and liberated the jews.

this soil is all of me.
my whole hearted history.

marauders and mystery.
in this life i was jolly.
but here i stand melancholy.

earth, my darling, you're the only home i ever knew.
so i wrote this poem just for you.

————————————————
————————————————

devin

————————————————
by robert gold
————————————————

dear devin,

in the heat of the night.
my heart flew, higher than the highest kite.

your chocolate skin.
lays just as smooth as your cali born kin.

in the heat of the night.
your mountains present a vivid sight.

your hips, your thighs.
a lie, to say these lustful antiquities are easily denied.

and the angels sigh.
a faint(ful) cry.
every time the boys grow shy.

cause such perfection,
should stand lifted, in heated affection.

————————————————
————————————————

to the tune of, 1, 2, freddy's coming for you
aka the ballad of, oh fuck i'm about to die

————————————————

by robert gold & joe pollock

knock knock...midnight strikes the clock.
one two...nobody knew.
what was waiting...waiting for you.

three four...heart full of gore.
better lock...lock your door.

five six...throw knives in the mix.
get cho...get cho pumped up kicks.

seven eight...don't fight your fate.
you're too late…you're at hell's gate.

nine ten...he just stabbed my friend ben.
freddy here's to kill again.

capturing the harp

by robert gold

the bows of cupid pierce my naked chest with the arrows of
love.
amadeus orchestrated fantastical tunes could make the angels
cry up above.

but what do the poets know of flirtation,
it's a game only known to the patient.

papers and pen cannot pontificate the passions of poe on
parchment to capture synchronicity.
aphrodite's wisdom is not a dictionary definition, because
writings and rhythms do not assimilate authenticity.

because even when my vocal inflections mirror and match
madonna.
lyrics, limericks and love tunes cannot lick nirvana.

plays, poems and presentational performances can practice and
practice.
yet absent the tried and true real life status.

stephanie meyers and dick clarke, sit humbly in the dark.
if such arrogant assholes assume they can capture the spark.

near sight-ed.
contrit-ed.

un-delight-ed.

because perfection is nice,
but real life is spice.

lucifer came as a snake.
er-rate.

it was fate.
for god's sake.

that adam and eve, the first two mates.
would eat the cake.

would seek out knowledge that the tree could offer.
because ignorance is to soffer.

and a fairyland filled with fake bliss.
is that nothing more than a santa claus kiss.

and the more i listen to this filth from the solicitors at my
doorstep,
proclaim and profess the lord and his rep.
the more i roll my eyes at the sheep and their shlep.

the more my pretty little gorgeous ear holes lay molested,
i fear individuality is dead and soberly rested.

and you know what really fucking bites my toe,
and makes me just wanna strangle a ho.

the hitlers and the hannibal's can bask in heaven and the
rapists and radicals can repent.
holy shet!
where have the solicitors minds went?

and yet you can burn in a holy hellish empire.
for feeding masturbatory sensual desire.
and hot lustful homosexual fire!

and i'm kinda angry at you god, because i think suppressing
indulgence and human nature is the true sin.
 in my perfect precious little opinion.

the exotic and the unique are the highest, the best.
and you crinkle and crumble and cry, foolish mortals there is
no test!

and so lucifer, seeing the error of his father's ways helped us
escape from paradise so that we could achieve knowledge.

creativity.
and achieve the ability.

to write literature.
to paint pictures.

to pontificate poems.
and build creepy garden gnomes.
and design unnecessarily large homes.

so calm on, calm down!
and turn that christ-ly frown, upside down.

you can smile, with your two front dimples.
cause i defy, that real life is all that simple.

and you can choose to call me a criterion.
but personally i say the apple had to be eaten.

to achieve read-in.
and elaborate eat-in.

and assigned seat-in.
and holiday greet-in.

its creativity.
its truth.

that satan gave to us.
and so i shall build his bust.

for the dark lord deserves it.
for he is the true poet.

he gave us the ability to write about love.
and sing beautiful songs.
and be creative and make oscar films.

and if we had stayed in new eden.
and the apple had remained uneaten.

we would not be who we are meant to be.
we would not be who we are today.

and whether or not the devil is real.

the religious right can take a breath and heal.

because darkness
is not the sword that he wields.

he's an instrumental genius.
and unlike god,
he encourages us to enjoy our penis.

he's a guitarist.
he's the tardis.

but most of all,
he's the first of the harpists.

---

pumped up kicks

---

by robert gold

---

the quiet child at the end of the hall.
holds a bullet in his bag for every and all.

he's upset, and depressed.
it needed no more or no less.

he's a mess.
with malevolence in his quest.

infuriation in his chest.
its human nature at its best.

fear struck the students, as he entered the class.
and as the shots fired, the ground hit the glass.

from being excluded from soccer,
and pushed into lockers.

nobody cared for the loner in the back of the bus.
no hand on his shoulder to say, "you're one of us."

and before he popped his own head, with led,
these were the words that he had said...

"in school i was the boy who had never spoken,
but you're the culprits who made me broken."

---

we'll speak the universal tongue

_____

by robert gold

_____

and from the very start, we shared places in each other's
hearts.
because while we're young, we'll speak the universal tongue.
they are the letters in the bottle; they are the sonnets of
aristotle.
and the cold hard touch of sorrow has no place to rest its
head.

because while we're young, we'll speak the universal tongue.
and it can be achieved from bliss, and it can be perceived
through a kiss.
and the cold hard touch of sorrow has no place to rest its
head.
because all the disperfections are dead, and no
disproportionate dispassion knows this bed.

and it can be achieved from bliss, and it can be perceived
through a kiss.
they are the letters in the bottle; they are the sonnets of
aristotle.
because all the disperfections are dead, and no
disproportionate dispassion knows this bed.
and from the very start, we shared places in each other's
hearts.

_____

_____

the ~~sophomore diaries~~
aka
tales of a 10th year nothing

_____

by robert gold

_____

let me bestow on you a story of an adolescent boy without a
strain of confidence.
but one day he learned to use his toys, and his life's been
different since.

deemed a virgin,
that much seemed certain.

but on his first day of his sophomore year,
the boy swallowed a strand of his childish fears.

he proclaimed, he would find a girl to take to the winter
forum.
she didn't have to be adorable just average and every day
normal.

and though it was already late november,
he still had to find a date by december.

finally in biology class,
he had found his hope at last.

a shy shell of a woman stepped into his life.
a lie to claim that she one day became his wife.

and for the duration of their high school career.
they kissed with bliss and shared some beers.

they sought out knowledge,
in the halls of college.

for a time they shared an apartment in upper manhattan.
he studied law while she learned latin.

rarely did they ever fight, cause he always knew that she was
right.
but when they did they never faltered to make love that very
night.

they often went out on the town,
in her best blue dress or a red ball gown.

two songbirds in a pool of affection.
before one day he threw it into dissension.

after one night at the bar,
he took home a blonde in his convertible car.

bringing a horrible ruin,
to a once great union.

and once his girl discovered his other fling.
down from the wall came a once beautiful mural.

decades have since past,
and he now knows happiness at long last.

now he's married and has three children.
a lawyer who lives in a two story building.

but every once in a while his memories bring him back to his
long past mom.
and the good old days, when she dressed him up for prom.

and as he flipped through the pages of his old yearbook.
he remembers the biology girl and the time she took.

_____
_____

a very sexy Valentine's day
_____

by robert gold
_____

and you know what's not a lie?
the fact that i die.

and i let out a sigh.
every time we say goodbye.

our kiss.
it's ultimate bliss.

you're magnificently fine.
and you take me to cloud nine.

but that's all the boring stuff.
i know how you like it rough.

and i think the angels cry.
every time you suck me dry.

and the truth is, absolutely yes!
i love your double d breasts.

but i'm sorry, i know it's quite a pinch.
that i can't give you a 12 inch.

does it make you somber?
that my hot dog isn't longer.

but, you knew exactly how to maneuver my penis.
honestly i think you're a genital genius.

i'm sorry i couldn't think of anything that rhymes with vagina.
so instead i'll be making you a pizz-ah-pie-ah.

but listen, look.
i can't cook.
but i can make you feel defiled.
i can shake you doggy style.

i have no hesitation.
to say you're a heavenly sensation.

please, say to me.
you'll always be my lady.

you evaporate all of my sorrow.
its happiness others wish to borrow.

if god made you in his own design.
then damn, the holy father must be fine.

but joking aside,
just give me an everlasting promise that you always remain
mine.

because, your perfection,
gives me a humongous erection.

you make me so grateful that i no longer have to jerk off, in a
sock.
because i finally have a place to put my cock.

and girl when you give me oral.
i lose all of my morals.

and your beauty is oh so divine.
and that's why i'm asking you to be my valentine.

————————————————
————————————————

to the tune of, a british guy

————————————————
by robert gold & joe pollock
————————————————

you're the school house rock.
and you've always been my rock.

you're the queen of them all.
you'll muse the next rohl dahl.

you'll breathe the next stephen meyers.
tv pilots, like pretty little liars.

you impassionate the picassos.
the argos. the flocos. the broncos.

i'm you're julius caesar.
and you're my cleopatra.

and it's a pleasure to meet yah.
imma lucky creature.

you're my yoko ono.
see another guy flirting, i say oh no!

you're my jane seymour.
bringin heirs to the floor.

you're the comet, that got it!
that left the dinosaurs in a coffin.

you're the slayer of kings.
hear that mama mantis sing!

you're my little wiggly figgly bibbity shmoobity clickety
clump. and might i say woman, you have quite a nice rump.

the perfect rump, practically a camel hump.
a backdoor baby bump, a lump that i love to watch take a dump.

you're my favorite crayon in the tickly toy box.
and you're my favorite place to rest my cocks.
[i have three, my great grandmother was a hermaphroditic
shark]

and when you ride me, you ride me like an ox.
and when you're not around i have to jizz in me socks.

i love to put me swimmers inside your bottom half.
you make me smile, and you give me a laugh.

you're the best thing that i've ever had.
and when you're not around, it makes me sad.
———————————————————
———————————————————

a love story of boys & rifles
———————————————————
by robert gold
———————————————————

flowers of the battlefield are so beautiful.
boys drenched with bullets to the bellyful.

blood of my forefathers.
redemption, nobody bothers.

in death we find only inadequacies.
red rivers of casualties.

blood spilled for future generations.
so we wear our military decorations.

finally boys find their aspirations.
their highest motivations.
patriotic affiliations.

rifles in the meadow.
to seek out our manifesto.

war drums to the tempo.
battle cries out chirp the sparrow.

for too long we have become a nation drowning in blood.
it's a catastrophic flood.
thousands dead in the mud.

history takes our boys off.
asking for deeds too rough.

out there young boys become men.
but history takes them time and time again.

so we say our amen.
hoping they'll be safe then.

though it doesn't do a damn thing when.
we get a body bag for ken.
and a casket for jenn?

after what i've seen.
soldiers as young as thirteen.

how could i ever believe?
that we are anything but killers.

so many lost.
is this what freedom costs?

and for what.
i raise this question to the almighty.
in his anger he can smite me.

why do young boys fight the wars of old men?
again and again and again.

———————————————
———————————————

mothers & sons,
and the tumultuous relationships which often follow
———————————————

by robert gold & joe pollock

---

this is a poem...in no uncertain terms.
so let's enjoy this moment, before we become food for the
worms.

wisdom, loyalty, and breath.
you gave me life, and you love me to death.

when you & i are not in zen,
can we become friends once again?

does momentary lapse of like, deter love?
is my momentarily hate masking pain?

did we waste too many years in vain?
screaming, yelling, crying, destroying.

i'm sorry if sometimes i can be a little bit annoying.
ripping, tearing, bleeding, breaking each other.

all in front of the eyes of my little brother.
but despite our turmoils, you're still my mother.

we're stronger. were better. were slightly fatter, but were
working on that.
this is love...in no uncertain terms.

And the winter snow

---

by robert gold

---

winter came,
and winter left me,
sullen in,
the deepest despair,
masses of,
a whimsical care,
winter kissed,
and winter cried,
winter saddened,
and winter lied,
winter stole,
so many truths,
winter loved,
and winter lost,
winter fared,
and winter quelled,
and winter's heart,

firmly swelled,
but winter was,
far too late,
winter was,
gone too soon,
gone again,
with the autumn bloom,
and winter was for-got-ten,
a year passed,
all again,
to the sight,
the sight of men,
and the winter snow,
was brought back,
back once,
back again.

—————————————
—————————————

black mirror
aka
the anti-intellectual society to which we find ourselves privy
to

—————————————
by robert gold & joe pollock
—————————————

sometimes you're blue
and sometimes you're red.

but are you even listening
to the words that i have said?

you've gotten lost
in your digital echo chambers,
and you've forgotten your friends.

there's a world outside,
bellowing with unswam ocean tides.

you walk through a library
like it's a museum.

asking, where are all my dog ear filters,
i don't see em?

but everything you do see,
in this library.

you say, not for me.
you can't handle that kind of intellectual autonomy.

cause you can't even handle a soft read.
through the filters of your eyes,

these books look like ancient relics.
but by now your minds, already drifted off
to your next amazon fedex.

these books,
to you,

look like a museum,
do not touch.

so eager to de-educate yourself.
what's the rush?

and you don't even know
that these are books to be consumed.

but what's the use,
your so obtuse,

you'll die,
not knowing that,

that black mirror
in your palm's a tomb.

and it's slowly sucking your brain juice,
and it's wrecking yah, till you look like ted cruz.

you're too busy working towards
your carpal tunnel.

while your cerebral's flown off
in one of elon's shuttles.

you fall asleep next to your phone,
like "he" deserves a cuddle.

like "he's" your only lover,
and you'll never find another.

and you'll remain forever a stranger to the works of poe,
whitman & langston hughes.

as you consume reality, and all your principalities, and every
aspect of your personality,

thru ur pal in your pocket,
and some may be offended that i'm knockin it.

but this wake,
this earthquake.

of technological fate.
has made you an anti-intellectual.

absolutely antithetical.
trepidatiously reprehensible.

and irredeemably anti-social.
and a manic going postal.

"i think it's just better if you leave me alone."
you substitute emotion and just live on your phone.

and in conclusion,
at the end of a long long hard day of texting

when your thumbs are raw,
and the bones of your hands

are all worn down.
so much so

that if i asked you to clap,
you couldn't even make the sound.

i would ask you one question,
one question,

for all the children of the land,
of uncle sam.

would you please follow me
on instagram?

---

flawless

---
by robert gold
---

when the days are long, and the headaches of hardship have
stolen harmony from my grasp.

the tune of your harp is all the placidity i need to find my
composure.

to bring the quietude of restfulness into the tranquility of
our union.
a humble bed of humble sheets of a reposed nature.

the beckoning of sweet nothings in my ear.
your whispers are provocative.

and yet even when your tantalizing words bring a sensual chill
down the nerves of my naked back.
the amorous exhilaration pulsating through the hairs of my skin
is gratified gradually.

your touch is subtle and slow in style.
i'm in love with a caitlyn, who used to be kyle.

---

love & other drugs

by robert gold

---

a hundred nights pass,
like a hundred years.

consumed by,
too many heartbroken tears.

has it been a century,
since you said it was over

or has this love lost penitentiary,
stolen my composure.

in complete honest sincerity,
you were happiness resurrection.

now desperation stares at me,
at the loss of life's perfection.

after our break-up
there was a time

when we tried
to rekindle our flame,

our fire,

our humble romance.

and we found ourselves
in the back

of your daddy's pickup,
absent shirts,

absent underwear,
absent pants.

but yet
even that

turned to nothing.
when I thought

maybe we were
rediscovering something.

because fate
wouldn't have us.

because 2 days later,
you got hit by a bus.

———————————————
———————————————

school ties

———————————————
by robert gold
———————————————

i know not the identity of a jew.
but still, it keeps the christians from loving you.

tell me boy, from what lands do you hail from,
as if that was your summarization and national anthem.

and ears scream with the hollowed echoes of christ killer.
even though these hands weren't the ones to pull the trigger.

not history's winner.
just a biblical sinner.

i know no moses or the prophet abraham.
but were grouped in together by uncle sam.

my name is robert gold
and the penny jokes, and getting kinda old.

———————————————

---

if i could drive

by joe pollock

---

i'm sorry i couldn't see you
i've been apologizing to you lately
if i could drive, you might even be happy to see me

at least i'd like to think so
it's been an ongoing theme

where i'm up all night about to scream
because i got lost in your eyes (again)
like fools gold in a diamond mine

too good to be true
every single time

but i have too much faith in the cliche
and everyone asks me why i stay

in a bubble of hollywood endings
i'm only a character in your life

i heard that somewhere before
not a lead, but supporting the idea that i'm what you're
looking for

if i could drive, i wouldn't have to dream anymore
well ... shit

---

lulu

by joe pollock

---

you were just a kid, dancing in the clouds
and so was i, usually acting out loud
i never really thought we'd be the best of friends
it was your party, but you died at the end
lulu

when i heard that you were gone
time was passing by too long
it's hard for me to remember you
oh my friend, lulu

i don't wanna fall too deep in a dream

68

where i can still hear you scream
it hurts, i know you're in pain
crying inside your untamed brain
i miss you, lulu

and i wish i could remember your smile
but i haven't seen you for a very long while
i feel so guilty not saying goodbye
it seems too easy to wave at the sky

(ending)
i miss you
i love you
i'll see you soon

_____
_____

a compliment in the moon river
_____
by joe pollock
_____

(prologue)
sweet woman
with the shiny shoes
hey woman
you're a phenomenon
sweet woman
let me bring you a rose and sing you a song

i am troubled
uncontrollably
by your belated reply

because….

i got stuck
in your cool jeweled smile
reflecting in the mirrored window

as a white trash bohemian
i am always looking for something good
while trying not to embarrass myself

your golden brown hair gets in the way of that
as i'm reminded of my infatuation with brigitte bardot and liz
taylor
leaving me tongue tied in another freak show of words

the reality is that you are a no bullshit kind of gal
that's what makes you as genuine as an old timey jazz riff

and as groovy as audrey hepburn in the moon river midnight

i never knew what it meant to be real....

a quality of ignorance haunts my dream to know a perfect girl
but when i open my eyes and it turns out to be true
no one could possibly be as great as you

---

pushing daisies

by joe pollock

johnny was fourteen, now he's pushing daisies
lola found out, now she's going crazy
eddie doesn't know, what mamas gonna say
well nothings been the same since jason moved away

i'm sitting at the table, i always eat alone
with one eye on the door, and wonder if they're coming home
i don't know what to say, i don't know what to write
my feelings are as crossed as i was last night

there is no thanksgiving, no bird prepared to share
i think i'm alone now, sitting in this chair
the television's on, but there's nothing on
there are no white horses or glorified love songs

another day goes by
i'm staying in tonight
sick and tired of watching
all my family die.
and ignoring the ones who are still alive
i don't know what to do
and don't know how to help
 maybe i can start
by working on myself

---

california boy

by joe pollock

your eyes
told lies
last night
outside
piss off
get lost

70

live free
with no cost
no luck
no love
just crying on the bus
my life
it sucks
because i'm feeling fucked
a california boy
who gets easily annoyed
and can't deny
i've tried
i've tried
to be more like you.
but maybe it's time
you learn
a little bit from me.
i'm a man without a class,
therefore
i've never seen a difference
between me
and the rest of the world
i never judged anybody
for anything
i love you all,
why can't you fucking love me?

---

city of psych

---

by joe pollock

---

wake up little sweethearts
now the monsters have been scared off
but the promise to act different has been thrown out the window

you've got your ticket to ride
i've got my mind in two heads
good god we look like goons
trying to make our own beds

you tried to be hip
and i tried to act cool
it was the craziest thing we ever tried to pull

said enough was enough
said he'd live at the pub
you should have thought things through
before you joined the club

you said no need to worry
you said the fire was out
i guess i was too young
before i had any doubt

you fought all the time
you both committed the crime
i thought it wasn't my fault
so who ever knew
i'd end up with you?!

i guess that's what it's like
when you fall off your bike
and your mother fucking frame of mind
diverted to the city of psych

scars

by joe pollock

i got drunk
and thought of love
nicotine's not good enough
is it too late to say i'm trying?
i got stuck
and tried to hide
i contemplated suicide
at a time i felt like dying

i lost a friend
a petty accident
i should feel better
but i still apologize for things that aren't my fault
it took some time
to realize it doesn't seem to matter
every time i leave, i don't know if i'm happy or sadder

if i sleep
i always dream
that freedoms just a fantasy
please tell me
if i'm being too dramatic
(i'm not sure if i like this poem anyway)

because i'm still me
unfortunately
but the writing helps a lot

12

to be quite clear,
i'm still here
apologize i will not

Born in november (affirmation)

by joe pollock

i never knew what it meant to be real
i was born with an imagination so explosive,
i could hardly handle it sometimes
i like to pretend that nothing bothers me
because who would want to listen to another sob story?
even if i did, would you take me seriously?
or would you force a smile
and fake a sympathetic tone for my benefit?

in reality, i'm humble in thought but weak in action
i'm a fool in a man's body
i've always spoke my mind and have never seen a problem with it
i can't speak for anyone else because they don't talk to me
anymore
because of this, i thought i was the bad guy

no longer the super hero my dad thinks i am
so i tried being someone else, but that nearly gave me a heart
attack
i lied to myself about myself
because i forgot what i was living for
i'm not here to be remembered, i'm here to be alive

i'm happy with who i am
no matter what gaslighting narcissist tells me
the reality is in fact;
i'm just a second class cripple from pacoima
from a long line of peasants, prostitutes and petty thieves
no gene pool, but a gene puddle somebody pissed in

and with that knowledge, i'm ready to say goodbye
to all the fuckers who looked at my fingers, instead of my eyes
it's ok, but i'm still not sorry
xx

---

sandpaper blues

by joe pollock & robert gold

73

i am the doctor—in his office, showing off my snaps to you.
you know you can be really beautiful.
you need not be a drag, we'll snip here.
tuck it there and pull it in between
we'll grab some glycerol from your gluteus, and give you some
big ol' knockers.
some chesticles that'll make the cows go moo.
you'll have the boys biting their knuckles, and wondering how
your milkshakes brought all the bois to the yard.
but damn right, it's making us all hard.
you'll have nails that'll make the harpies jealous,
so long, they'll leave every motel finger bang lookin like a
scene outta dexter's masturbatory diary.
you'll have collagen lips, and fill out that pink moist face
vagina like an animal zoo balloon.
you'll look like a million bucks. you'll look so money all the
south korean cosmetic surgeons will claim responsibility for
you.
you'll be an orphan no longer, because every doctor from soho
to seoul will claim credit for birthing your beauty into
existence.
you're gonna look like a barbie doll sweetheart, so stop
screaming, take my laughing gas, and let me place my knife on
your face in all the appropriate places.

_____

_____

scream
_____

by joe pollock & robert gold
_____

she smoked her way into abandoned love
drugs did her good, but it wasn't enough
she guilted me, made me pay for it
what a dirty soul, i couldn't handle that shit
her father was a bigot and her mother was a drunk
both held in high regard because we love them
psychedelics were her thing but it's still not enough
it just makes me wanna scream

(music plays)

she used to be a model, was addicted to cocaine
i guess it's just an 80's drug, so everything's okay
i don't know why she's screaming
"everything's my fault!"
"it'll go back to normal soon, i promise
nothings been the same at all

that was then and this is now, (1996)

74

a couple kids later, now her dress doesn't fit
anxiety was a memory but it's back to haunt her heart

in l.a, she used to get fucked up
skid row downtown, she was always junked up
behind closed doors, there's 2 kids that she ignores
trying to impress, with blinding eagerness
she's got a dirty mouth smelling like a cigarette
cashing welfare checks, going into debt
she's guilting me, making me pay for it
what a dirty soul acting perfect
god damn, i ain't paying shit

she's a damn dirty harlot, on a needle a day.
she's making me car sick, as she pumps up her vein.
her daddy's singing koon, like a deadwood saloon.
she's a mother of two, but she looks like a fool.
but we still love her, no matter what they say
a catfish a day, keeps the doctor away.

(music stops)

_____
_____

for jane

_____
by joe pollock
_____

verse
red wine stains in the pouring rain
when i feel you in my heart
i'm sorry for the fights you heard next door
it was toxic from the start
you didn't get to see me become a man
stand on my own and start a band

chorus
i wish i wasn't scared to say goodbye
i hope i die one of these nights
so i could hug you
because i'm thinking of you
i miss you baby
baby jane
i miss you baby
baby jane

verse
i don't wanna cry about yesterday
in this intoxicated state
and i'm gonna try to find my way

without waking up in pain
you died near thanksgiving in paradise
took your last breath and closed your eyes

chorus
i wish i wasn't scared to say goodbye
i hope i die one of these nights
so i could hug you
because i'm thinking of you
i miss you baby
baby jane
i miss you baby
baby jane x2

_____
_____

whatever

_____
by joe pollock
_____

(verse)
talk about worry, im crazy in a hurry, everything's going
blurry
i'm going nowhere
i sing songs in the city for those girls too pretty, and that
untamed love of mine
i'm going nowhere
never saw it coming, thought it was just another woman
riding shotgun all alone

(pre chorus)
i'm going nowhere
i'm going nowhere
i'm going nowhere

(chorus)
because i tried to socialize with a different crowd
saying something stupid right out loud
i should be pissed to be so defined
whatever! whatever!
mom and dad don't mind!

(verse)
just a heartburn sinner, a hypocritical winner
with broken hearts and promises
i'm going nowhere
nothing else to do, i haven't got a clue
just waiting for my weirdo bliss
i'm going nowhere
another day wishing, with the same fuckin vision

where my cab ran out of gas

(pre chorus)
i'm going nowhere
i'm going nowhere
i'm going nowhere

(chorus)
because i tried to socialize with a different crowd
saying something stupid right out loud
i should be pissed to be so defined
whatever! whatever!
mom and dad won't mind!

(verse)
i keep my heart wide open, i am still fuckin hopin
that this time won't be a lie
i'm going nowhere
it's nobody's fault, a poor excuse
except for mine

(pre chorus)
i'm going nowhere
i'm going nowhere
i'm going nowhere

(chorus)
because i tried to socialize, with a different crowd
saying something stupid, right out fuckin loud
i should be pissed to be so defined
whatever! whatever!
mom and dad won't mind!

_____
_____

a savage self realization of the american dream
_____
by joe pollock
_____

Do you have the same problem I have? I'm not talking about
life. I'm talking about regular day situations. Like the times
when you think your only friend is the TV. And he's always
trying to sell me something. one of these days I feel like he's
gonna jump out of there and shout; "Hey do you want this?!" Do
you know what I'm gonna say? "Do I look like a sucker asshole?"
Do you think I'd buy something from a guy who is perfect? From
a guy who has perfect hair and perfect teeth and stands next to
a girl who is perfect? Do you really think I'd buy something
from a guy who tells me if I buy whatever the hell he's trying
to sell me, my life is going to be perfect? Is that reality?!

11

At a decently teenaged part of life we tend to lose our innocence. I think we get wrapped up with bathroom smoke breaks and trying to keep up with the prom queen. People will smoke anything only to find comfort in themselves. Not realizing they forgot what it means to have ambitions and goals. We forget who we are and forget how as an individual we were going to change the world. No matter how small.

There have been many times when I wanted to give up because I didn't believe in myself. My ego had died but not before stripping away my innocence from unhappy humans, you know the bullshit spewing-kind. I was self aware, and I wasn't to be messed with. I learned when I was young I had been bullied by the greatest tease. She wasn't a woman but she existed. She was life. My self realization of this fact made me understand what it was like to have a place in the universe that didn't feel bad for me. I was reintroduced to music, movies and culture. As a young teen I saw many different points of views than I had earlier in age. At the right old age of 15, I had become my own man.

When I was in high school, my biggest problem was that my teachers would teach me that a certain subject exists but they wouldn't tell me how to use it. So I immediately started to resent them and found an education in my own personal library. Hunter Thompson said, "There is no such thing as paranoia. Your worst fears can come true at any moment." Applying my own personal attitude I think he meant we need to stop worrying and just do it because the only thing stopping you from doing what you wanna do, is doing it. A fear of incompletion will just make it worse. When you're in school and it seems like somethings going in one ear and out the other, try to take time to understand. If someone isn't helping your growth, make it your goal to do it yourself.

"I wanna be discovered!" Is what some of us may say. But this is planet Earth! The unpredictable romantic comedy that's gonna break your heart. But for some reason you and everybody here is addicted to that heartbreak. You have to take what you can get. With whatever you get, make it your own. You can't stand around waiting for something to happen. Do you know how easy it is to say, "I wanna be a movie star?" But actually going out and working to do that. The do it yourself process that we all wish we can hire someone to do for us.

Another day's dream through hell and back might make us want to question the meaning of life and whether there is a higher power in this world. Whether it be called God or just a force in the universe, either way whatever we give, we take away more. Sometimes religion can't help us. No matter what that good book says, it's gotta come from the human nature that we all share with each other. It's up to us to make the peace of our minds. In the long run, God isn't gonna save your ass.

There's a common saying, "If you've got God, you've got a friend." Switch that phrase around and I believe in that saying, "If you've got a friend, you've got God." Love and community is what it takes to keep one's dream alive. Hard work is only defined by the people who work everyday. But if you're following a dream it shouldn't feel like work. Choose your love. Choose your life. Choose the cherry on top because as my old mentor brad koepenick says, "Magic is real!"

At this millennial age everything is gonna seem like it's the end of the world. But it's not. All the crap that's in what I call the dirt box. Whether it's a rejection, a breakup, a bad grade, an eviction, an asshole for a president, it doesn't matter. What matters is whether you choose to be the hero of your anguish and pick yourself up and take all the crap that's in your dirt box and throw it out the window or not. If you do, you can keep moving forward. Somewhere in your life you'll have a dream come true and a song that sings.

---

to set a scene ...

by joe pollock

An old gas guzzling, black rust bucket of a pontiac bounces down on the homeless side of Los Feliz. In the front seat are two young guys - one blonde white dude and a brown haired fella. Both wearing cheap thrift store suits with thin black ties. Their names are Vincent Ego and Jason Rolla. Everyone calls vincent by his last name. Jason is behind the wheel.

They stop at a Beverly Hills mansion and gaze before getting out. Jason steps out to the trunk to take out a couple of 45 automatics. Ego sits in the passenger seat as Jason cocks his gun and conceals it in his jacket. He tosses the other to ego to do the same.

With their matching suits looking like someone's prom date, Jason and Ego walk through the courtyard of what looks like Errol Flynn's old Hollywood home. They walk all the way through the yard and enter the lobby to make their way up the dreaded staircase.

As they reach the end of the stairs and now looking for a certain room, they start pacing back and forth. They pass a pink door which seems to be the right one. Jason knocks on the door and cracks his neck like whatever they're about to do is a regular gig.

A girl named Maggie answers in confusion having never seen these dudes before. They enter a room with the girl and two others waiting. These three young girls get caught off guard. Maggie, the blonde young girl, who opened the door and who will, as the scene progresses, remain crisscrossed on the bed.

Selena, a sorta preppy girl just waiting for the wild energy to come out.

Hannah, a jeans and t-shirt type of gal who has yet to say a word, sits at the table with a big sloppy piece of pizza in her hand. Ego and Jason walk in there like they own the joint with their hands in their pockets and their chins up held high. Jason is the one who does the talking.

As Jason and Hannah start to talk, Ego sits down with the two other girls. Jason takes out a letter explaining to Hannah that he has to kill her and the girls. Actually just her but now that there are now witnesses, him and Ego have to do what needs to be done. She begs for mercy out of the scary confusing letter. She has no idea what she has done. Jason takes pity on her and kidnaps her instead.

As they walk out of the room, Ego shoots the two other girls with no expression on his face whatsoever.

Fade to black.

_____
_____

day dreams

_____
by joe pollock
_____

verse
high school mornings turn to sleepless nights
cryin' break me out of this misery
won't take much to kill a teenage dream
and if i wake up in morning i just want to scream

chorus

take it back, it's not the same
make a plan to live without the blame
choose to live, find a way
everything and nothing comes to a delay
in day dreams!

verse
gettin' on the bus, breaking from the wild
i wanna live a good life, i wanna come back with a smile
redeem
before the week in hell decides to go extreme

take it back, it's not the same
make a plan to live without the blame
choose to live, find a way
everything and nothing comes to a delay
in day dreams!

someone come on and cry me a prayer
if i'm sinning will you even care?
i've been kicked in the face for too long
hoping everyday that i can stand up strong

take it back, it's not the same
choose to live, find a way
everything and nothing
and nothing, always finds a way

_____
_____

you wanna fuck my best friend

_____
by joe pollock
_____

i heard you don't really like me
you were just pretending
i think it's really funny
you wanna fuck my best friend
'cause he is not interested

now both of us are crying...
we're crying

everyday it's something different
last week you had a boyfriend
now it's not important
i wish you would ignore him
but that would get him interested

jesus, can i catch a break yet?
why can't i get a girlfriend?
i never thought that was important
but i'm getting kind of restless
i've been a slut for a while now...

like russell brand or something

will i lose another best friend?
or will i lose your courtship?
this piss contest is pointless
i guess i'll write a script

one where you two get together and die at the end
you know you both deserved it
i'll regret it in the morning,
but you're an easy target

xx

_____
_____
The end of the world will be just fine
_____
by joe pollock
_____

kill me first and kill me fast
time moves like an hourglass
they're trying to hide the proof
they run away from the truth

all the questions i did not ask
you make sure i finish last
i don't know why we're so shy
but i'm tired of all the lies

let them know we're here to stay
we're here to fight another day
be the hero in your story
mother earths eternal glory

kill me slow and kill me quick
we're suffering in the apocalypse
what's it's gonna take to see
to see the hungry get enough to eat

no place to come home
living in the danger zone

(ahahaha)

the cold city night

by joe pollock

there's a big open car
but i can't drive that far
cause the assholes i fight
they all beat me with fright

and they bully my heart
it's a breaking apart
yeah they fuck with my head
till i'm just good as dead

in the cold city night

i feel lost in a maze
can't get out of this craze
i need help from my friends
one more missed call again

there's too much going on
i'm depressed and i'm gone
but i hide in the back
so the kids won't talk smack

in the cold city night

there's a tv that screws
there's no netflix to choose
but a hundred news shows
that do not amuse

and i'm walking around
feeling lost but not found
gotta pick myself up
before i die in the ground

in the cold city night

spin the bottle

by joe pollock & robert gold

it's that time again this year, i'm feeling kind of lonely
it's ok, i'm doing fine, there is no need to worry

friday nights have been so crazy, i've been drunk since
november
i haven't seen your face since, oh shit, i can't remember

i met you when you were dating that sexy guitar player
i almost said i love you in front of him and other sayers

i often wonder how you're living in your fairy tale ending
i wish you would come back and say "i was just pretending!"

it was perfect when we were naked, here i go again
i'm still nostalgic, i hope that you don't tell your friends

our first kiss was created, by a silly party game
your boyfriend watched us and laughed, musicians are all the
same

jimmy wasn't jealous, but he kept his eye on me
i still called you and you still answered me

one last spin is the most i could ever ask
i know it's just a fantasy, let's see if we make this last

one last spin, let's see where it will land
if this is what i think it is, jimmy's out the band

three years pass, and you're a memory of my past.
haven't said your name out loud, since last december mass.

wherever you are, i hope you're doing well.
driving in your car, eloped in heaven's hell.

i hope the next guy that you meet,
loves you more than me.

i realize now, i gave too many thoughts to you, this is me in
retrospect.
here lied a clown, who was stuck on you, a genuine genuflect.

i gave too many thoughts to thots,
a practice this brain wroughts.

you bring toxic men around,
that screech like morning hellhounds.

you're like a walking advertisement for what women shouldn't
be, your everlasting torment and raged toxicity.

if your life was a like film, you'd be no country for good men.
and so all i can offer you, is this paper and this pen.

---

cool

---

by joe pollock

---

the dream to be a rockstar is still more or less the same
i'm trying to remember what you said to make me stay
in your eyes i'm a moron, the only one to blame
i still cry and try to hide from your charming devil ways
oh, i was dumb, a lonely one, i still am
i fell in love with nicotine like idiots do
and thought i was cool
but i'm sitting here alone, wondering where my friends are
i thought that i looked cool, but i don't look cool to me.
truth is i never felt this before till now,
i don't feel cool anymore…

5:53

---

by joe pollock

---

it's 5:53 in the morning
and i'm still lying in bed
sarcastically imaging a life before we met
my mother always said
it's best if we're not friends
i never knew what she meant
i just didn't understand

as time went by
i tried it once and tried it twice
my friends and i are feeling very nice
it's nice to unwind
anxiety's a memory,
and no one else seems to mind

as years go on,
teeth fall out and hair grows long
my dad moved back to england
and my brother joined him soon after...

i moved into a trailer
at 5:53, i'm more awake than ever

the smoke is clearing away
unfortunate circumstances elude me to think
i wish i had more time, who knows when i'll die
doesn't matter why,
 i wish i had more time

if i knew life was gonna be this hard
i would have fucking tried,
but it's alright
i'm like a character on a soap opera
they keep trying to kill me off,
but i'm the only one bringing the good ratings

you ain't ever getting rid of me
xx

_____
_____

it was just a stroke
_____
by joe pollock
_____

i am crooked, just a little bit
it's been a burden, i hate to admit it

oh poor baby, i was innocent
drill a screw now, place it in my foot

hammer it in
and see if i'll walk straight

i was born dead, a happy accident
i'm still standing, despite your ignorance

almost killed me, i will never quit
i've been limping, don't ask me again

what's my problem, it's only you who cares
it's pretty simple, it was just a stroke

i am crippled, i don't care that much
despite my movement, i do not need a crutch
forget my fingers, look into my eyes

_____
_____

when
_____
by joe pollock
_____

and so it last, it came to pass

i only caught a glimpse
and it was gone again
reached to grasp and felt it pass
grabbed at the air
it's gone again
i saw the glow, bathed in warmth
and left with chills
i'm gone again

suddenly a train of thought pulled into the destination
heading towards the dark side, but i've already been
if not now, then when?
if not then, then what can you tell me?
and then again, it comes around
a chance to smile
fuck, it's gone again
if not now, then what can you tell me?

---
as the world turns
---
by joe pollock
---

as the world turns
it's fear that grabs you, not devotion
as the world turns
 dollar signs spin off their axis
say it ain't so, so it ain't
as the world turns
fear brokers stuff their mattress
as the world turns
it burns so bright with me
as the world turns
it leaves you cold without feeling
say it ain't so, so it ain't

as the world turns
be careful not to drop your phone
as the world turns
be warned, your heart might ache
say it ain't so, so it ain't
as the world turns
alliteration doesn't make up for substance
say it ain't so, so it ain't

as the world turns
lust is the fuel for perpetual motion
as the world turns
see your heroes fail

as the world turns
roll the dice and play the game
as the world turns
does it make you smile?
say it ain't so, so it ain't

_____
_____

start over
_____
by joe pollock
_____

lately things have been a mess
seems like my whole world is full of stress
with scary voices everywhere
i can't breathe this kind of air

i do my best to act real cool
pretending i'm not a dumb fool
and that ain't nothing i can fix
awkwardness is how it is

i walk the streets an empty teen
i've lost all sense of what i've seen
i live and yet i do not feel
each day gets more and more surreal

i do except i've done some wrong
it's up to me to be self strong
i'll be trying all the time
and see if that gets me my life

maybe one day
i'll be okay
if i just breathe in
and just start over

_____
_____

forget it
_____
by joe pollock
_____

(verse)
my mom warned me, yes she warned me
that i'd meet a girl like you
she also told me heart breaks' stupid
but you gotta do what you do
i could have taken you to the movies
so nervous that i would shake
but now that dream seems to fade away...

88

i wish i could bring it back
=
(chorus)
but i'll be alright
just get out of my sight
don't wanna see you again
forget it
forget it
don't get too full of yourself

(verse)
friends told me to just forget it
"she never liked you anyway!"
but i could never be the friend
 who sits in the backseat
riding shotgun all the time just isn't enough
i got to make my way into the driver's seat
take a leap of faith
it'll be worth the heartbreak

chorus
but i'll be alright
just get out of my sight
don't wanna see you again
forget it
forget it
don't get too full of yourself

(verse)
whatever happened to "i like you, hey do you like me too?"
every time i start self loathing
i begin to think of you
we could pretend we never met
but then i don't know what you'd do
you could wait and realize that you're with a stupid jerk
but when you come to look for me
i'll say you're just berzerk

(chorus)
but i'll be alright
just get out of my sight
don't wanna see you again
forget it
forget it
don't get too full of yourself
_____
_____

broken house

_____
by joe pollock
_____

there are rats in the walls
birds flying in the halls
there's bad history everywhere
and i'm locked inside
it's hard to smile like it's nothing

i don't want to lie

staying home in bed all day
when i can't see, i can't sleep, i can't breathe
you don't care about what i say
so you ignore me
unfortunately

_____

_____

kicking through the ashes

_____
by joe pollock
_____

kicking through the ashes of a funeral pyre looking for a trace
of a once bright fire. that burnt so hot it scorched the soul,
it burnt so bright beyond it's whole.

kicking through the ashes of a funeral pyre, born of forbidden
love and true desire. died a death that was slow & amp;
tortured slowly and feeling cramped.

i've been kicked through the ashes of a funeral pyre.
resurrection feels a lot like pots, and forks and fryers.

that flame it flickered but now is out.
so there's nothing left to cry about.

_____

_____

in my dreams

_____
by joe pollock
_____

tell me something, don't be shy
don't be afraid, you don't have to hide
i'm just crazy, thinking about you

if you find yourself too deep
i'll dig you out and take the leap
you're like my favorite song stuck on the radio…

any day, i do not care
love sometimes just isn't fair
if i could buy the world i'd give it all to you…

a kiss on the cheek, if you don't mind
i'll be led on in good time
what would happen if that was a crime?

i'll tell the truth, i've loved you all this time
everyday since i met you......

'cause you're in my dreams
you're the angel who guides me through
when you're in my dreams
you're the one who's saving my life

i won't wait up for you xx

―――――――――――――

―――――――――――――

no man's land

―――――――――――――

by joe pollock

―――――――――――――

life is supposed to be fun
something you can't outrun
as i'm walking down the town all i see are the guns
when you're going through hell and crawlin' out the back
taking all the jokes
you're called a maniac

well i'm not gonna cry, no that would be mad
i don't wanna belong to the bipolar fad
because i've seen all of that
and i don't care if it's true
because i've got all my dreams that i wanna pursue

now my sins are my own
i can't break free
from my own crazy mind i call reality
people say damn it
but i can't commit
to being the educated hypocrite

traffic lights and shopping carts
punctured lungs and broken hearts
in no man's land
epileptic shocks like lightning
wake up dumb, it's so annoying
in no man's land

thank god i'm not thinking about her
oh shit, i am now
i acted like an idiot
these poems are all the same, but damn man,
these are real feelings

i'm scared of myself and i romanticize things
how unfortunate that i'm drunk, so i think i sound smart
but what if it sounds like gibberish to the general public?
fuck it, no more self doubt
do i say that too much?
wait, wasn't this about the girl?
about love and other stuff
how much more can you take of this?
how much more can i take of this?

jesus christ, it's interesting
this theory we call shame
i learn a lot from it, my favorite teacher in many ways
i'm doing better now than i ever did in school
i've always learned better by myself

which is probably why i didn't get into college and barely
graduated high school
oh those poor teachers, i meant no offense
but i stand by myself telling the vice principle to fuck off
because he didn't understand me

it's not his fault, i was younger then
but i get the feeling he'd say the same thing to me again if
the bastard had the chance
i've always been bad with numbers, test scores is what matters
whoever told you that probably keeps a calculator up their ass

i'll never like those people
because we don't know each other, separate worlds,
does that sound like a story line to a disney channel original
film?
that's a trick question….
of course it fucking does

i'm afraid to keep talking, because i don't know when this ends

92

i always think and think and think
it's easier to talk to myself because i think i'm the only one
who listens
at this moment, i'm having a panic attack over the possibility
of someone reading this

i have nothing to hide, not ever
i think it's just narcissism because i want people, or at least
someone to see it
am i self indulgent? i see no shame in that
for years i thought i was a narcissist but i'm only just
determined

writing might be the very one and only thing i'm actually good
at
i've been inspired by many assholes
because they taught me
if you love someone you learn to ignore people's flaws and bad
habits

what about my intolerance for people who yell at me, make fun
of me and use me for money?
so of course i am determined
no more hangin' out with bullshitters
and i'll fucking keep going
i don't know how to end this
is this long enough?

_____
_____

one shot

_____
by joe pollock
_____

(verse)
i got thrown on my ass on a summer day, stuck in the rut of
life
slept in the park where i used to play,
only tried to stay alive
smoked a cigarette, it got in my eyes
from then on i was blind

(chorus)
don't let your lack of vision
put you in this situation
one shot of self depression
another day of nervous aggression
one shot of total perfection
another step in the other direction

(verse)
woke up distressed, in my friends old room
eviction happens way too soon
saw a girl i liked, she was with her man
infatuated til i die

(chorus)
don't let your lack of vision
put you in this situation
one shot of self depression
another day of nervous aggression
one shot of total perfection
another step in the other direction

(bridge)
it's a curse, for the worst, i'm going mad
another day in a dream
it's no ones fault, except for mine
gotta own up to this crime

(chorus)
don't let your lack of vision
put you in this situation
one shot of self depression
another day of nervous aggression
one shot of total perfection
another step in the other direction

(ending)
one shot!
one shot!
one shot!

_____
_____

liz and dick
_____
by joe pollock
_____

crooked in love
you're just as bad as each other

and you're crying on the floor
circumstances change because the dream come true you once
invented,
was intoxicated by reality and false promises

this mistake happens quite often
lovers fall down unsure whether they should get back up

we cannot settle for the worst and believe this is the best we
can do
trust the love, but don't be naïve

your heart will break a thousand times
but in that, you shall find pieces of yourself

but never let anyone tell you that your crazy
because you're not

you've been secretly playing a game
a game i like to call liz and dick

that's where one of them screws the other one over
and the other one retaliates and does it back to them.

but then they realize they're just a couple of blind pigs who
have no idea what the hell they're doing.

i guess that's what they call love. it's full of mistakes.

but that's life, as they always told me.
you can do it over and over and over again.

---

light up my day

---

by joe pollock

(verse)
these words i write are pointless here
to say what i feel inside
compliments of desperate desire
can hardly make sense of these lies
the poet has tried and he's failed bad
ive gone and i've wasted time

(chorus)
all i can say
she lights up my day
all i can say
she lights up my day

(verse)
the stupidity of happiness
is more or less the same
she held my hand when i was stuck
left me with nothing to say
the message is clear and i'm stuck down here

i cannot ignite her flame

(chorus)
all i can say
she lights up my day
all i can say
she lights up my day

(bridge)
she lights up my day
she blows me away
she'll cut my heart open and leave me empty

(chorus)
all i can say
she lights up my day
all i can say
she lights up my day

(fade)

_____
_____

am i happy?

_____
by joe pollock
_____

i'm a second class person, citizen wise.
this is something i must recognize.

it's not my place to make a complaint, but am i happy?
no i ain't!

i missed my chance when i was young, now i live below the
bottom rung.

i was put on this earth to discover my knack... now i want my
money back!

why should i do good when i'm misunderstood? i really wish i
could.

so why don't you ask?
when it comes to a costume i'm left without a mask.

even if i wasn't i ain't got no need to have it and even if i
did, i'm just a teenage kid....consequently

_____
_____

fright or be frightened

by joe pollock

i got nothin' to do in this old town
i'm gonna go out and punch a clown
i can't be square, so i gotta be cool
it's fright or be frightened

somethings smacking like a bully
and it's creeping like a shadow

as the tv keeps hold of the laughter
it's time to go on and go hereafter
it's the show that takes hold of control
each channel and your every goal
the one that takes your very soul
light or enlighten

fright or be frightened oh yes yes yes
fright or be frightened

you were born quite very capable
but this maze might not be escapable
you hear the roaring in the cave
so bite or be bitten
there is no brightness at the end
no graduation to attend
no welfare money you have to spend
like a cheap house mom who must pretend
and it's breaking my very heart

hell it's the real world, that's what it is
fright or be frightened
light or enlighten
bite or be bitten!

the world is crap and the world is cheap
might as well put yourself to sleep
we all have tried so many times
it doesn't seem to right our crimes
it's just a world for the distinguished
oh, it's just a world for the distinguished
fright or be frightened
light or enlighten

stronger than the rapid tides
or grieving from the suicides
and the girls are calling in a cloudy night

the girl is calling on a cloudy night

she says fright you crazy scary boys
fright you crazy scary boys
fright or be frightened
light or enlighten
bite or be bitten!

_____

_____

satisfied
_____
by joe pollock
_____

(verse)
you wanted control of your heart and your soul
you wanted your head to be clear
but history came back to haunt some old sins
now you're screaming and drowning in tears

(pre)
whatever happened to acting the fool with no worry and laughing
all night?
whatever happened to feeling as free as the tide?

(chorus)
were we sad inside?
where we sat in time
were we satisfied?
watching our lives go by

(verse)
i can recall when you used to walk tall
like a man without fear in his head
now you're confused, feeling lost and alone
with the weight of the world on your back

(pre)
whatever happened to acting the fool with no worry and laughing
all night?
whatever happened to feeling as free as the tide?

(chorus)
were we sad inside?
where we sat in time
were we satisfied?
watching our lives go by

(verse)
open your eyes, take a good look and find

something you're missing inside
i'll answer your calls if you drop down and fall
i'll help you however i can

(pre)
whatever happened to acting the fool with no worry and laughing all night?
whatever happened to feeling as free as the tide?

(chorus)
were we sad inside?
where we sat in time
were we satisfied?
watching our lives go by

we were satisfied
we were satisfied
we were satisfied....

---

explanation of an idiot

by joe pollock

I'm sorry about the other night
I got too excited
All I wanted was to impress you
But I really fucked up
I'll admit, there was pressure
Boys can be really cruel at times
(It wasn't on purpose)
But I still feel guilty

Everything I strive to be is the opposite of how I acted
I'd like to blame the alcohol
But that would be too easy
The best excuse I could think of
Is that I really like you
I felt you were one of the few that could actually understand me
But I got scared
I'm tired of excuses

Thinking my "sensitive side" would get me out of trouble
Fuck me, when did that ever help anyone?
I feel like I should be the one who gets killed first in a horror film
I'm a fool in a man's body

I yearn for a second chance
Even though I know it's too late
I think I've been watching too many romantic comedies
Believing in a happy ending
But I don't live in Hollywood

I swear, I'm not the asshole you might think I am
I just haven't learned how to talk to you yet
That doesnt make me stupid,
I just haven't met anyone like you

First impressions can be deceiving
Maybe that's why most people prefer to text
To hide how embarrassing they can be in real life
Can you tell me why I'm so scared?
Scared of you and what you might think?
I don't know how to stop
There is no preconceived notion,
You'll probably tell me to fuck off
Everything I've told you is the truth
If you still don't believe me, that's alright
You've taught me so much
It makes up for the rejection

I won't make the same mistake.

_____
_____

the meaning of love

_____
by joe pollock
_____

love makes you interesting
it makes the world you live in real
love shows you what it truly means to feel
love makes you crazy
love makes you question everything you want in life

love is a tool
love is a drug
love is a fool
love is a bug
love can be strong
and make you hate yourself
(but i love it)

love makes you know you are not alone
it's most people's motivation
because...
there are enough aspiring actors in the world

love is a whore
that makes you pay for it
love is the things we say
and can't take back

love is bipolar
love is the night
love makes you blind
love makes you fly
love makes you fall,
(but i love it)

love makes you want to shower
just so you can get dirty again
love doesn't apologize
love might laugh at you
love makes you disbelieve and believe again
love is accepting love

love is shattered glass you should probably avoid
love makes you bleed
love is a song that makes you cry
love shows you no mercy
because love is an asshole
(but i love it)

love is like telling me you're a healthy alcoholic
addicted to the special effects
then we wake up and regret sunday
love is waking up at noon and doing nothing all day except
watching cartoons and smoking weed

love is motel sex

love is your mother pointing a knife at her stomach when she
doesn't know what else to do
love is your dad calling you a waste of space when he's
frustrated
love is your grandma who drinks too much
love is your nana kissing your hands
love is your grandpa who you never got to know
love is smoking cigarettes with the grandpa who you do know
love is your auntie who can't remember your name
love is uncles who don't quite understand you but love you more
for it

love is knowing that you're fucked up

and understand this fucked up shit
help me and i'll help you
it's a wicked world but we gotta share it

love is me
love is her
love is him and love is you
love is everyone in between

love is everything...
and i fuckin' love it

(mic drop)

_____
_____

(my)
colossal fuck ups
you most certainly might make
as well

_____
by joe pollock
_____

Asking a girl if you can kiss her
(There's nothing less romantic, you just gotta go for it)
Kissing your best friends ex
Asking said ex out on a date
Getting too attached
Mistaking infatuation for something more

Saying I hate you when you wanna say I love you
Saying I love you when you wanna say I hate you
Calling in sick when all you want is an extra hour of sleep
Giving away your money out of fear of being lonely
Being alone and wanting to go back to the bastards who made you
feel like shit

Forgetting a lie you told
Lying when you can't back it up
Lying in general
Acting like an idiot when all you want to do is impress someone
Trying to act cool so you can make a certain kind of friend

Believing you're not enough
Wishing you were someone else because you think you'd get what
you want if you were them
Believing everyone else is better than you when you have no
idea what's going on in their lives

Apologizing for not knowing how to help

Apologizing for not knowing how to do something when you just
haven't learned how to do it yet
Dancing around an uncomfortable subject
Not asking for help when you really fucking need it

Wanting more when you don't know what you have
Wanting to be famous
Drinking more than you can drink
Smoking more than you can smoke
Not knowing when to stop
Telling people you're fine when you really aren't
(I guess that just brings us back to lying)

Not saying thank you when someone properly saves your ass
Sharing something that your friend asked you to keep private
Thinking you peaked in high school
Mistaking laziness for your "shitty life"

Mistaking your acquaintances as friends
Caring way too much about someone who clearly doesn't give a
shit about you
Forgetting to bring a condom when you know sex is guaranteed
Being arrogant and full of yourself when you're way off base

Ignoring the good things you say about yourself
And ignoring the bad things that follow

(Because that's how you recognize yourself and get good again)
_____
_____

afterword

_____
_____

I would like to let you in on my thought process as a writer.

Self-publishing my own books is a creative project that I
endeavored upon when COVID started, as I felt that something
good needed to come out of so much bad. And when quarantine was
over, I wanted to feel like I had done something productive
during my time of social isolation, which doesn't have to
necessarily be a curse, but a blessing in disguise, as it
serves as an opportunity for us to do the things we normally
feel we don't have time for; like our music, our dancing, even
our writing, now that the world has slowed down. When the world
is moving so fast, all the time, we all feel like there's no

time to endeavor into creative projects that may not pay dividends.

The yin and yang part of me felt like wallowing in the FUCK 2020 mindset just wasn't healthy. I had heard people say that phrase just 4 years prior. FUCK 2016. It seemed as if every time something in the universe outside of our control happened, it had to personally affect me. But I rejected that notion, feeling it my mission to make 2020 a great year. And to this point, I still have both my legs and arms, and 2 eyeballs, and thus I have to say 2020 has been my best year yet.

In addition to the accomplishment of not losing any ligaments, I've now self-published 3 books. A novel, *How to Lose & Influence Nobody*, a short self-help book, *The Laws of Practical Application*, and of course, this book of poetry, which as I am writing this, I currently do not know the title.

My writing partner Joe & I are considering several, in fact I've talked him into possibly allowing me to indulge myself and release several additions on this poetry book, all with different fonts for the poetry as well as entirely different book covers and even book titles.

Marketing a book can be difficult and I don't know which title will best catch on with an audience. I'm also conflicted whether funny poetry or serious poetry is the way to go. I think both can exist simultaneously together but of course, the advice I always get is that a poetry book should stick to a common theme. Although since this is an afterword you probably already know that my poetry goes off on a number of different topics. And if a collection of poetry published in one book is supposed to be on a single topic, you can certainly call this little creative endeavor a tangent.

Alas, I will have to leave it up to you to decide whether this amalgamation of poetry is suited for human eyes.

-- September 3, 2020
Robert Gold

Printed in Great Britain
by Amazon